HAUNTED HOTELS

KEN HUDNALL AND SHARON HUDNALL

OMEGA PRESS
EL PASO, TEXAS

HAUNTED HOTELS

OMEGA PRESS

An imprint of Omega Communications Group, Inc.

For information contact:

Omega Press

5823 N. Mesa, #839

El Paso, Texas 79912

Or http://www.kenhudnall.com

FIRST EDITION

Printed in the United States of America

OTHER WORKS BY THE SAME AUTHOR
FROM OMEGA PRESS

MANHATTAN CONSPIRACY SERIES
Blood on the Apple
Capitol Crimes
Angel of Death

THE OCCULT CONNECTION
UFOs, Secret Societies and Ancient Gods
The Hidden Race
Flying Saucers
UFOs and the Supernatural
UFOs and Secret Societies
UFOs and Ancient Gods
Evidence of Alien Contact
Secrets of Dulce
Intervention

SHADOW WARS
Shadow Rulers

DARKNESS
When Darkness Falls
Fear The Darkness

SPIRITS OF THE BORDER
(with Connie Wang)
The History and Mystery of El Paso Del Norte
The History and Mystery of Fort Bliss, Texas

(with Sharon Hudnall)
The History and Mystery of the Rio Grande
The history and Mystery of New Mexico
The History and Mystery of the Lone Star State
The History and Mystery of Arizona

The History and Mystery of Tombstone, AZ
The History and Mystery of Colorado
Echoes of the Past
El Paso: A City of Secrets
Tales From The Nightshift
The History and Mystery of Sin City
The History and Mystery of Concordia
Military Ghosts
Restless Spirits
School Spirits
The History and Mystery of San Elizario, Texas

THE ESTATE SALE MURDERS

Dead Man's Diary

OTHER WORKS

Northwood Conspiracy

No Safe Haven; Homeland Insecurity

Where No Car Has Gone Before

Seventy Years and No Losses:

The History of the Sun Bowl

How Not To Get Published

Vampires, Werewolves and Things
That Go Bump In The Night

Even Paranoids Have Enemies

Criminal Law for Laymen

Understanding Business Law

Language of the Law

Border Escapades of Billy The Kid

PUBLISHED BY PAJA BOOKS

The Occult Connection: Unidentified Flying Objects

DEDICATION

As with all of my books, I could not have completed this book if not for my lovely wife, Sharon.

TABLE OF CONTENTS

PREFACE

If the reader has done any traveling at all across this great land, he r she has stayed in a hotel or a motel or an Inn or a Bed and Breakfast. Whatver it may be called, these establishments have served the needs of people since before the formation of this country. Howver, in the darkness of the hallways and corridors of these historic establishments are numerous stories of hauntings. So read these stories and remember that whenever you travel away from home overnight, you may be spending the night with unexpected guests..

TEXAS

Hotel Paso Del Norte

101 South El Paso Street

El Paso, Texas 79901

Figure 1: Hotel Paso Del Norte (CAmino Real Hotel)

The Hotel Paso Del Norte was the dream of Zack T. White, a native of Amhurst County, Virginia, who became a successful El Paso businessman. Ironically, the design of this historic hotel was the product of two great disasters, the burning of El Paso's Grand Central Hotel in 1892, a well-known four-story structure that had been located on the site of the present-day Mills Building, and the 1906 San Francisco earthquake[1].

Zack T. White had been one of those who had helped try to extinguish the fire at the Grand Central Hotel and recalled this incident as the beginning of his idea to build a fire proof hotel in El Paso[2]. After the 1906 San Francisco earthquake, Zack White and J.E. Lewis, an engineer, copied the foundation plans and the design features of those buildings that had survived the quake. These earthquake proof features coupled with a fireproof design were incorporated into the Hotel Paso Del Norte (the Hotel on the Pass to the North), which opened for guests in December 1912.

Of course, the Paso Del Norte was not White's only contribution to El Paso. He aided in the building of the first Santa Fe Street International Bridge, which was replaced by the Paso Del Norte Bridge in 1967. He helped build the first brick plant in El Paso as well as the first streetcar line. He served as Vice President of the Gas, Electric Light and Power Company. He was one of El Paso's strongest advocates for the use of electricity and gas. But he is most remembered for the building of his "dream hotel."

---

[1] Jones, Harriot Howze, El Paso: A Centennial Report, A Project of the El Paso County Historical Society, Superior Printing Inc, Texas 1972.
[2] Ibid

The Paso del Norte was built on the site formerly occupied by the Kohlberg Cigar Store and Factory, the Guarantee Shoe Store and the Happy Hour Theatre, El Paso's best known vaudeville house. It took two years for the 1.5 million dollar building to be completed by Trost and Trost Architects[3] and J.E. Lewis, the construction engineer. Only the finest materials were used in the construction of Mr. White's "dream hotel" as he desired that the hotel would be the finest constructed building in El Paso at the time and for many years to come. The ten-story structure was built of steel and concrete on an earthquake-proof foundation, with a brick exterior and terra cotta trim. The inside partitions and walls were made from "fire-proof" white gypsum from nearby White Sands.

The lobby was designed with a meticulous attention to detail, Mr. White had Italian artisans brought to El Paso to do the work he wanted. He had Tiffany's of New York specially design and construct the golden Tiffany stained glass dome with its elaborate mahogany carvings that graces the lobby of this grand old hotel. The dome is actually made up of seventeen pieces and is suspended by

---

[3] Englebrecht, Lloyd C. and June-Marie, Henry C. Trost, Architect of the Southwest, El Paso Public Library Associates, 1981.

wires due to the tremendous weight, which would otherwise collapse in the center.

The Dome Bar Chandeliers are unique in their design. During one of the renovations of the hotel, these European chandeliers were installed to light the lobby. These electrically lit fixtures were among the first electrical lights in the area. The chandeliers in the Dome Restaurant, which was originally called The Depot, are replicas of the original candle chandeliers that were lowered in the evening for the candles to be lit and then raised back to their normal height. There were actually three lobbies in the original design, each decorated with cherry stone, green and golden scagiola, lit by European chandeliers and trimmed with black, serpentine marble. It was truly the finest hotel of its type in the country. This showplace opened on Thanksgiving Day of the year 1912 with a very lavish ball.

Over the years the roof top ballroom and patio were the scenes of many dinner dances and Sunday tea dances. It was also the preferred gathering place for those who wanted to watch the progress of Pancho Villa's forces across the river in Juarez during the Mexican Revolution. Later is became the center of the cattle industry, with more cattle being bought and sold in the lobby of this hotel than any other single location in the world.

This historic old hotel remained in the White family until 1970 when TGK Investment Co., Ltd. bought the structure from Mary and Katherine White, the daughters of Zack T. White. There have been several renovations and remodelings of the Paso Del Norte, the most recent major change being the addition of the 17-story tower in 1986.

Zack White wanted to build the most modern hotel in the southwest. Therefore, on December 19, 1912, he had a huge oil storage tank installed in the Hotel Paso Del Norte[4]. The tank, manufactured by the El Paso Foundry, was 8 feet in diameter and 62 feet long. It was constructed to hold 12,100 gallons of oil to be used for heating the hotel. The plan was for the tank to be filled directly from railroad tank cars on the G.H. & S.A. tracks through a pipeline built directly to the hotel.

The original hotel used coal to fire the boilers that provided steam heat to the rooms. The coal would be collected in rail cars and dumped on the yard adjacent to the property. In 1915, the Hotel Paso Del Norte built a coal bin underneath the hotel in which the coal would be placed

---

[4] From an unpublished history of the Camino Real Hotel loaned to the author.

instead of leaving it out in the weather. Interestingly enough, the coal bin was built next to the hotel bakery.

The original design of the hotel did not have closets in the rooms. Instead, guests would use cloakrooms with hooks mounted on the walls to hold their clothing. This was done because in those days, most travelers would carry their clothing rolled up in large carpet bags. When the traveler would arrive at their destination, they would unroll the garments and hang them on hooks. This is why the rooms in the old section of the hotel offer mahogany armoires instead of closets for the use of the guests. There is no question that Zack White spared no expense in ensuring that the Paso Del Norte was a thoroughly modern hotel. Another unusual feature of this magnificent hotel was the installing in the basement of tiled hot tubs and bathing areas for use by the guests.

Of course, I am sure that Mr. White had no plans for his hotel to become a haven for the restless spirits of those who have not yet gone on to wherever it is that the dead go, however, almost from the first, guests, employees and staff have seen and heard things that are beyond the ordinary and the expected. I am told that some people refuse to stay in the old sections of the hotel due to unusual occurrences.

I have attended many events that this historic old hotel, and naturally, in idle discussion with other attendees at these various functions, the conversation has often turned to the stories association with the old hotel. For example, I heard that a young woman wearing a long white dress has been seen in the basement of this hotel, by members of the staff.

According to the story associated with this ghost girl, she had gotten pregnant and thus it was agreed that she and her young man would get married. As both families were somewhat prominent in the community, arrangements were made that this wedding, that was to take place on the tenth floor of the hotel, would be one of the first events to take place at the newly completed Hotel Paso del Norte. The wedding was apparently the social event of the season and everyone looked forward to it, especially the pregnant girl. When the big day arrived, everyone was at the hotel, except the groom. He never showed up. Mortified and depressed at being left at the altar, the young would-be bride jumped to her death from one of the tenth floor windows. It is said that it is her spirit that comes back looking for her young man. This author met her in the elevator and she looked as real as can be.

On the mezzanine, is has been said that sometimes, usually late at night or in the early hours of the new day, members of the cleaning crew will see a door where there has not been a door before. When they get close to the mysterious door and listen, the sounds of a party can be clearly heard coming from behind the door. No one, as of yet, I am told, has opened the door to see what is beyond it. Rather, those who say they have seen the mysterious door have gone to get someone else to witness this rather bizarre situation. When they return, the door and the sounds emanating from behind it have vanished. They find only blank wall where the door had been only a short time before. Perhaps, one day, someone will have the courage to jerk open that mysterious door and see what is lurking behind it – or will they?

Zack T. White's original Hotel Paso del Norte has been added onto several times over the years. The current entrance and Registration Desk is in the new addition. In 1986, the Dome Bar was built, directly beneath the exquisite Tiffany Dome for which the hotel is so known. As a result of this conversion of the lobby area into a bar, the original entrance to the hotel now opens directly into the Dome Bar and is rarely used. Another of the expansions to the original Hotel Paso del Norte resulted in the demolishing of the Ellanay Theater, a historic old theater that had been built in 1918, by J.M. Lewis and Victor Andreas, at the cost of $94,500.00. The Ellanay opened to great fanfare on November 10, 1918 with a seating capacity of 940.

Many came to the Ellanay just to see the unbelievably ornate façade. The two owners had spared no expense in trying to outdo all of the other similar enterprises in the city. There was a recessed arch over the marquee that enclosed a glazed tile mural featuring three muses from Greek mythology and two paired couples dressed in Roman clothing. Tree foliage formed the foreground under the arch and a Renaissance landscape in the background completed the eye-catching mural. The figures and the foreground were in bas-relief. The glazed tiles were large, about 24" square. The entire arch was approximately 25' in length. About four feet below the cornice of the building were busts of J.M. Lewis and Victor Andreas. Unfortunately, the 1983 expansion of the Hotel Paso del Norte resulted in the destruction of this beautiful old building.

There is another entrance into what used to be the original Hotel Paso Del Norte Bar, now called Uptowns, from San Antonio Street that is also almost always locked.

As a result, the historic original bar, which sometimes is opened for parties and political events, is seldom used.

At one event my wife and I attended at the hotel, which is now known as the Camino Real Hotel, we were early and the doors to the ballroom on the Mezzanine, where the event was to be held, were still locked so the staff would finish setting up the room. So we went to the Dome Bar to wait. While we were sitting there, I idly asked the cocktail waitress about a story I had heard of people walking out of the wall in the lobby. She smiled for a moment and looked around the bar. We were early enough that there weren't too many people about, so she balanced her tray against one hip and told us the following story:

"Well, I heard that there is a mural on the wall showing a group of people standing around a piano." I had never really noticed the mural before, I have to admit; however, I have two friends who tell me that they have seen the mural the young lady was referring to.

"I heard that one night," she went on in a lower voice, "one of the night managers was checking the bar, and comparing sales against stock levels, things like that. He began to feel like something was wrong and he glanced up to see a woman walk out of the mural and stop in the middle of the floor. He described her as young, slim and attractive. She was dressed in clothing from years ago and he said she was wearing one of those big hats with flowers on it. The woman looked around like she was confused or something and never seemed to notice the night manager standing only a few feet away. He went around the bar and started toward her, but she backed up right into that mural. He went over and ran his hands over the wall, but there was no place she could have gone. He suddenly remembered a job he had to do elsewhere and left the bar."

I asked if she had been seen again, and the young lady said it was rumored that some of the housekeeping staff had seen her once or twice walk out of the mural, but they had rarely stayed to see what the lady did after that. More than one worker, she said, had quit after seeing some of the things that happened in the hotel. She had not personally witnessed anything, but still, she heard a lot of stories that made her a little afraid to work the night shift in the bar.

Deciding to see if I could verify the stories that I had heard, I went to the hotel and asked to speak to the manager. I was directed to a lovely young lady by the name of Michelle L. Kaip, CMP, who is the Director of Sales. She very kindly took time out of her busy schedule to tell me the stories that she had heard since coming to the Camino Real.

I frankly expected a blanket denial that there were any ghosts at the Camino Real Hotel, however, Ms. Kaip was very frank with me. She said that she has heard folklore concerning two prominent spirits who have appeared from time to time at the property. The best known story, she said was about a young woman in a white gown. According to what she had been told, the girl was to be married at the Hotel Paso Del Norte but something happened and now she haunts the 10th floor. I asked if she had any idea of the name of the ghost and she said that it was rumored to be Katherine White, daughter of Zack T, White.

The other spirit that seemed to frequent the hotel is a well-dressed man who wears a black suit cut in the style of the 19th century and always wears a bowler hat. This figure has been seen a number of time and is rumored to be Ben S. Dowell, a Kentuckian, which became El Paso's first mayor. She added that Ben Dowell's home and saloon stood at 115 S. El Paso Street, coincidentally, the spot where the Hotel Paso Del Norte's original bar was built. I asked for examples of his appearances and she said that she had heard from housekeeping that he has the habit of appearing in closets and other odd places, scaring the daylights out of the housekeeper who comes upon him unexpectedly.

I asked about the stories that I had heard about doors suddenly appearing on the Mezzanine Level. She said that she had heard from Housekeeping that unexplained doorways and stairways have appeared at different locations throughout the hotel where there may have once been a door or stairway that does not exist today. She had not heard the story that I related to her of a housekeeper hearing a party going on behind one of the closed doors.

I then asked about the mural around the Dome Bar where the lady allegedly walked out of the wall. She replied that she knew of a large photograph but not a mural in the bar area. She said that there is faded artwork in what was the 10th floor ballroom, but she could not think of any murals in the lobby area.

I asked about seeing the artwork in the ballroom and she replied that it was no longer open to the public as what was the original ballroom is now an engineering room. Talking of the engineering department reminded her of a story that a friend had told her. She said that this was a man she knew well who had worked in the Engineering

Department. He had been in the Dome Bar one day when the man in the bowler hat came into the bar and sat down beside him. Her friend said that they had a very nice conversation of some length. He seriously thought he was talking to a guest until the man in the bowler hat had gotten up from his seat, walked into the corner near the bar and vanished. She was very confident that he was a credible witness.

I asked about other stories she had heard since joining the staff and she said that most of them dealt with occurrences on the 10th floor or in the lobby, though, as she had mentioned earlier in our conversation, the housekeepers talk of the man with the bowler hat appearing in various places around the hotel.

In retrospect, it is not a wild notion to think that the Hotel Paso Del Hotel, or the Camino Real, to call it by its' current name, could or would be haunted. Much life and death in El Paso over the almost one hundred years the hotel has stood has been associated with this imposing structure. Due to its' location, the Hotel Paso Del Norte was the virtual center of life in early El Paso. The photograph below is a re-enactment done in 1966 of the April 14, 1881 famous "Four Men Shot Dead in Five

Seconds"

Figure 2: Location of the shootout that left 5 men dead in 5 seconds

shootout took place in front of the Hotel Paso Del Norte. In this confrontation, Dallas Stoudenmire, the newly appointed city marshal, was called upon to deal with the murder of a former Texas Ranger named Krempkau by Johnny Hale, manager of the Manning's' ranch and a man on trial already for the murder of two Mexicans. Some of the testimony at the trial had been in Spanish and Krempkau had acted as translator for the court. Hale didn't like what was said and chose to accost Krempkau during the noon recess with a hidden gun that had been smuggled to him by friends.

So in this famous shootout, Johnny Hale killed Krempkau. Stoudenmire pulled his weapons and shot at Hale, but killing a man named Lopez, an innocent bystander. Then he fired again and killed Hale. George Campbell, ex-city marshal and an enemy of Stoudenmire chose to draw on the marshal. Stoudenmire killed Campbell. Of such confusion, legends are made and the death of an innocent man is forgotten.

Ms. Kaip graciously allowed me to wander the hotel and talk to some of the staff. A very cute young lady, Rosemary Coigoy, working at the front desk had a story about a guest staying on the 16th floor, directly below the Presidential Suite on the 17th floor. She was working the graveyard shift one night and the guest called to complain that the noisy party and the loud piano music coming from the floor above were keeping him awake. Security was dispatched to the suite, but it was empty, there was no party and no one was playing the Grand Piano in the Presidential Suite. However, at the same time, in the room below the sounds of the party could still be heard.

I then talked to Robert Diaz, Director of Security for the Hotel. He related two incidents that he had been involved in during his time on the job. A new manager that had been transferred to El Paso was living in the Hotel while looking for a house. One afternoon, she and her daughter went to the pool on the 10th floor. Upon her arrival at the pool, she saw someone she thought was suspicious, a lady who appeared extremely angry. She stood outside the only door to the pool area and called down to Security. Two officers were dispatched to check on the lady. When they arrived there was no one in the pool area. Assuming that she may have gotten out and left by way of the stairs, they checked the stairs all the way to the street level but never found anyone. She could not have gotten out of the pool area without being seen.

The other incident happened during the construction of the new floors. There was night security furnished by the contractor to make sure that the tools were safe. One night he was called by Hotel Security personnel and told that the security furnished by the contractor had run off of the job and that one man had kept running in he got to the street. They were unable to find that particular man who had been the one to spark the panic.

Finally, the guard that had disappeared was found and questioned. He said that his job had been to provide security for the seventeenth floor. He said that he was been warned not to shut the doors along the hall as they had all just been painted and it was fear that they would stick shut. Workers' tools were stored in several rooms so he was to just sit in the hallway and make sure that no one got into the rooms and stole any of the tools. He said that he had been sitting by a window reading a book when one of the doors, being held open by a doorstop, suddenly slammed shut. He got up, opened the door and replaced the doorstop and then went back to his book.

In a few minutes, he glanced back up to see the doorstop from one of the doors slide across the floor and that door slammed shut. Curious, thinking a friend might be playing a joke on him he reopened the door, replaced the doorstop and searched the entire floor, but found no one. He went back to his book and all was peaceful for a few minutes and then in unison, every door slammed shut. At that point he had panicked, and run screaming down the stairs. The guard on the sixteenth floor had heard him run by and he started running down the stairs behind him and then the guard on the fifteenth floor also started to run behind them. All he knew for sure was that he was not going back in that building.

In another incident, it seems during the construction in the 1990s, a crane fell from the roof, taking a worker along with it. The crane and the worker had crashed into the roof of the third floor. The only way to get the dead worker off of the roof of the third floor was to take him through one of the guest rooms. From that time forth, no one wants to stay in that room and from time to time, those in the offices in the part of the third floors where the crane crashed will hear something slam into the roof above them.

The Cortez Building

310 N. Mesa
El Paso, Texas 79901

Figure 3: Cortez Building (Hotel Vendome)

Located on the northeast corner of North Mesa Street and Mills Avenue, the 11-story Cortez Building began its life as the Hotel Vendome. The structure takes the shape of an L-shaped block about the second story, with twelve bays facing Mesa and ten bays facing Mills[5]. While this building was never ranked as one of Trost's more artistic designs, it did incorporate one original feature not found in other buildings of the period. Peering out of the roundels above the Mesa Street entrance is a series of portrait heads of conquistadors.

The hotel was erected at a cost of $1,500,000.00 for Alzina Orndorff de Groff, a hotel operator in Tucson and El Paso. This new hotel, to be called the Hotel Orndorff, was the third hotel to bear that name and the second Orndorff Hotel to occupy that same spot of land. It has been said that between the cost of building the hotel and the rich furnishings that Alzina Orndorff de Groff spent $6,000,000.00[6].

One week before the opening of the grand Orndorff Hotel in 1926, Alzina Orndroff de Groff was caught in a freak rainstorm, came down with pneumonia and died before the grand opening so had so looked forward to. Even so, it is said by some that she still watches over her dream hotel. Changes are unwelcome in this hotel.

---

[5] Jones, Harriot Howze, El Paso: A Centennial Report, A Project of the El Paso County Historical Society, Superior Printing Inc, Texas 1972.

[6] Ligon, III, Andrew J. *Haunting behind Scenes: Cultural Sports Grapple With Ghosts*, El Paso Herald Post, October 31, 1996.

In the lobby, workers have maintained that they feel the presence of others even when they are alone and most feel that these presences come and go up and down the stairs. There have been reports of reflections of people being seen in the gleaming metal work of the elevators who are not in the elevators. Connie Wang used to go through the building with the El Paso Ghost Tour and was very friendly with the security guard. One day she saw him walk past her without speaking and round the corner in one of the halls. She followed him to see if something was wrong, but when she rounded the corner, only seconds later, the hallway was empty, she found out later that he had not been at work that day, he was home ill. So what or who had she seen?

Children have been seen and heard playing in the hallways when there are no children in the building. How about Joseph, the little boy who loves to ride his cycle in the lobby area. If approached he will race around the corner and vanish, much the same way as the guard Connie Wang saw.

There was once a fast food restaurant located in one of the retail areas of the building. The night crew would complain of people coming to the counter, placing and order and then vanishing when the worker turned to fill the order. I am told that some employees refused to work the night shift.

In the ballroom of this grand building, a young woman dressed in a ball gown from another era sitting weeping, but if she is approached she rises and walks into the shadows where there is no doorway, but she disappears. Was this perhaps once a doorway that is no more? It has been theorized that at this location there is a portal to another dimension where once wedding and parties were held. Perhaps some of these entities are caught in between worlds, so to speak, doomed forever to try and get back to their home but always failing. There are reports of a room off of the cloakroom where there seems to be some type of portal or energy vortex. Several psychics have called this a doorway, but a doorway to where.

CALIFORNIA

Queen Mary

Figure 4: Th4e Queen mary in permanent drydock

The keel was laid for the HMS Queen Mary in 1930 at Clyde, Scotland, but was not completed until 1936 due to a downturn in the economy. She made her maiden voyage on May 27 of that same year. She served three years as a passenger liner carrying passengers across the Atlantic until war broke out in 1939.

Figure 5: The model room - contains numerous large scale models

When the United States entered the war, she was converted to a troop ship. Painted grey to make her more difficult to detect, she was known as the "Grey Ghost." She ferried troops from the U.S. to England in perparation for D-Day. During this time she set the record for the most people on an ocean voyage at one time with 16,683 people.

After the war she continued to serve the military by trasporting war brides and the children from Europe to the United States. She made 13 voyages in this capacity before she was refurbished and retured to passenger liner service.

By the 1960s ocean liners were falling out of fashion with the rise of air traffic between the continents. She made occaisional luxury cruises before being sold to the city of Long Beach in 1967. She made her final transatlantic crossing she was permanently docked. Her boilers were removed and she was rendered unable to move under her own power. She was converted into a hotel and museum.

Ghost Stories

There are numerous ghosts and hauntings reported on the Queen Mary, we are going to list only a few.

Figure 6: Passenger corridor

Stateroom B340 is no longer rented out because the the volume of paranormal activity. Some people claim that it is haunted by the ghost of a murdered pursur, but we found that information on other ghost websites and not on any of the tours conducted by the Queen Mary. The faucets are supposed to turn on by themselves, and sheets from the bed are said to have flown across the room. The room is now stark white with very little firniture in it.

Figure 7: Lobby of the Queen Mary

One of the most famous ghosts of the Queen Mary is believed to be that of John Pedder, a fireman in the engine room who was crushed by the infamous "Door 13" in the part of the ship known as "Shaft Alley." Apparently during emergencies, the watertight doors would be closed to seal off sections of the ship to avoid sinking. The legend goes that crew members would hop back and forth through the doorways as many times as they could before the door would close. John Pedder apparantly tried one too many times and was crushed by the closing door.

A man seen wearing blue overalls sometimes described as having a beard has been seen walking down shaft alley and disappearing at Door 13. On the Ghost and

Legends tour they refer to this man as "Half Hatch Harry," but that was not the real name. John Pedder is listed on the sign in the infirmary of crew members that died.

Figure 8: A famous passenger

The First Class Swimming Pool is another famous haunted location on the Queen Mary. Some reports claim that it is haunted by the ghost of people who drowned in the pool, but the Queen Mary's own sign detailing the causes of death for passengers on the liner does not list a single death due to drowning. The ghosts seen in the first class swimming pool seem to be exclusively female. There are reports of at least one adult woman and a little girl that haunt this location. The little girl is said to have drowned in the second class swimming pool (which has since been removed). Her name is reported to be "Jackie," and she is seen in many places across the ship.

Figure 9: Upper deck of the Queen Mary

The changing rooms at the back of the swimming pool are said to hold a vortex of negative energy, or perhaps a gateway between dimensions. One story suggests that this is due to a woman having been raped in the changing rooms at one point. There is a live ghost webcam that continuously films the swimming pool. The pool is also part of the special effects tour Ghosts and Legends of the Queen Mary which includes smoke and light effects.

While all of the boilers have been removed from the ship when it was docked at Long Beach, the massive rooms that once housed them remain. The forward boiler rooms are now used as part of the Ghost and Legends special effects show, the massive middle boiler rooms have been converted into conference space, and the aft boiler rooms are included on the regular tour and the late night paranormal tours. The boiler rooms were dangerous places, and it is not surprising that these locations may have there own ghost stories. Jackie is sometimes seen in the boiler rooms, as well as a male ghost that is thought to have been a crew member that worked on the boilers. The rooms are very massive and have a creepy feeling to them.

During World War II when the Queen Mary was known as the Grey Ghost, she accidently rammed one of her escort ships causing it to sink. At the point on the bow of the Queen Mary where she collided with the escort screams can sometimes be heard. The public is normally only allowed to visit this part of the ship on the Ghosts and Legends tour.

There are many other parts of the Queen Mary that are said to be haunted. It seems the whole ship is a beacon for paranormal activity. The infirmary and the Lounge are other parts of the ship with their own tales of ghosts. In our interviews with various members of the crew, we got reports of strange feelings fairly often. The only crewmember who reported seeing a possible apprarition related this story to us.

One waitress at the Chelsea restaurant states that she had been working the host podium and saw three guests walk towards her through the long hallway that leads from the deck to the restaurant. She looked down at the reservation book for a party of three, but when she looked back up there were only two people. She asked the guests whether or not they prefered to wait for their third member before being seated, but they said that there were only the two of them. She also reported that the faucets in the nearby womans bathroom go on and off by themselves.

NEW MEXICO

Desert Sands Motel

5000 Central Avenue, SE
Albuquerque, New Mexico

The Desert Sands Motel was built in 1957 and is comprised of 67 rooms on two floors. Once described as a first class facility in the 1960s, this motel has certainly seen better days. As has happened to many formerly top notch motels, it is now living out its days as a resting place for drifters and those with little disposable income. It also appears to be the resting place for many unseen residences.

The Desert Sands Motel is now ranked number 116 in a ranking of hotels/motels in Albuquerque. On the other hand it is a cheap and easy place to stay when you're headed west on Interstate 40.

THE HAUNTINGS

Several guests who stayed in the corner room on the first floor of the center building have reported that they had some very unusual things happen to them. Several said that almost as soon as they had entered their room and put their bags down on the bed, unusual things began to happen. There were cold spots in some parts of the room and unexplainable voices were heard coming from the bathroom.

In addition to the mysterious voices, the water in the bathroom ran by itself and the TV in the room kept turning on and off on its own. As if this was not bad enough, when it was not turning itself off, the television set was also changing channels by itself. The final straw for these guests was when the outside door kept unlocking of its own accord.

Radisson Hotel

Albuquerque, New Mexico

As might be expected of a city with the age and history of Albuquerque, there are a large number of hotels and motels available to potential travelers. In addition to indoor plumbing, some of the rooms even come with live in spirits. One such hotel is the Radisson.

THE GHOSTS

There have been a large number of unusual happenings reported as taking place inside this hotel. Some have reported that while staying on the first floor of the hotel they have heard peculiar scratching noises and the loud slamming of doors from the floor above, even if there was no one renting the room above them.

Others have talked of stories that they have heard about loud yelling and screaming coming from rooms that are vacant and sometimes women who stay in some of these rooms report being shaken from a deep sleep by what seems to feel like children's hands.

All of the floors have been remodeled except the third floor. In fact, guests are not normally permitted on the third floor. A few hardy souls who have been able to gain access to this floor report that as soon as the elevator doors opened they were hit with a gust of hot air. As they walked further along the hallway on this floor there is an area that was originally outfitted as a bar. The top of the bar itself is in perfect condition but the rest of it is completely destroyed. Several individual who have had the opportunity to get into this area report that in the corner of the bar was what appears to be newly broken glass. No one had an explanation for the broken glass as the staff rarely goes into the area and none of the windows were broken.

Ramada Hotel

Albuquerque, New Mexico

The Ramada Hotel in Albuquerque is another hotel with a somewhat unusual past and some permanent guests who are not registered at the front desk.

THE GHOSTS

According to some of the hotel staff, one of the spirits resides on the first floor of this large hotel. She said to be a very pretty young broken hearted lady, who was murdered in one of the first floor corner rooms by her lover who wanted her out of his life. She is said to only be on the bottom floor of the hotel, dividing her time between the hotel lobby and the corner room where she was killed.

More than one chamber maid has reported the when housekeeping goes to clean the corner room where the young was murdered that invariably find it in disarray. Among the things reported to have been found in this room are the bed sheets torn off of the bed and thrown onto the floor, the television set knocked onto the floor and the curtains torn from the curtain rods.

This type of activity went on so long in this particular room that finally, the hotel management just closed off the room and do not even make it available for guests. However, out of curiosity, periodically, the staff still visits the room. They always find it is a shambles.

Miss Gail's Inn

300 South Main Street
Aztec, NM 87410

Built in 1907 by George Stone, this building housed the first hotel in Aztec. Upon entering Miss Gail's Inn, you enter a time long forgotten of country charm and creatively

Figure 10: Miss Gail's Inn.

decorated theme rooms. Located downstairs in this two-story hotel are Rooms 1 through 4, the main foyer, and Giovanni's Restaurant where one can have an exceptional home-made lunch from 11am to 2pm, or Italian Specialty Dinner from

6pm to 9pm by reservation only on Friday and Saturday evenings only.

THE GHOSTS

There are several ghosts that are said to occupy Miss Gail's Inn. One spirit is that of a lady who is seen to float down the stairs. Room number seven, located on the second floor of this historic old hotel is occupied on a sort of permanent basis by a very cantankerous old man.

There is a tree growing in front of the hotel that was used as a hanging tree in the early days. It is said that from time to time, bodies can still be seen swinging in the wind from the limbs of this old tree.

Holy Cross Sanatorium

Deming, New Mexico

The Holy Cross Sanatorium was located on part of what had been known as Camp Cody. The U.S. War Department in 1917 established a 2000-acre training camp near the town of Deming, New Mexico during World War One. The garrison of soldiers assigned to this base, called Camp Cody, was made up of National Guardsmen from Nebraska, Iowa, Minnesota and the Dakotas.

Official opening of Camp Deming was on December 29, 1916. The day was marked with a flag raising ceremony. The camp was renamed in honor of William "Buffalo Bill" Cody on July 20, 1917. William Cody was born February 26, 1846 and died on January 10, 1917.

The 34th Infantry Division was called the "Sunshine" Division at first, but this was in conflict with the 40th Division formed at Camp Kearney, California at the same time. So Camp Cody's 34th became known as the "Sandstorm" Division. Base quarters were built for 36,000 soldiers and the hospital had 800 beds. Camp Cody closed on June 20, 1919.

When World War One ended, the facilities at Camp Cody were converted for use as a tuberculosis sanitarium for ex-soldiers. Later the buildings on Camp Cody were turned over to the Catholic Sisters of the Holy Cross who continued to operate the Sanatorium. In 1939 most of the other buildings on Camp Cody were destroyed by fire. It was also about this same time that the Sisters decided to close the Sanitarium.

In the mid 70's there was a devil-worshiping cult that used the abandoned Sanitarium as the site for their rituals and the sacrifice of animals. There is currently only one building still remaining on the site, the others having either burned in 1939 or been torn down due to deterioration.

THE GHOSTS

There are many who maintain that the one remaining building is definitely haunted. Many intrepid individuals who have explored this old building have heard noises from the upper floor and seen lights near the fountain at night.

There are stories that tunnels run from this building in the northwestern part of town to the southeastern side of town. It is claimed that the tunnels come out at the airport. As is usually the case, these tunnels were discovered by the local teens and used as a party place. As a result, most of them have been caved in to keep trespassers out.

A number of people have claimed to have experienced something in the part of the old building referred to as the "Altar Room". Several people have said that they have seen a shadowy figure lurking just inside the doorway. The sound of footsteps also echoes through the empty hallways.

There is also a cemetery just to the north of the building. Some of the old graves have been disturbed and a large cross has been cut down. There is an urban legend in Deming that holds that all of the teenagers involved in cutting down the cross in the 70's all died that same year.

The hauntings are also said to not be contained within the walls of the old Sanitarium, but to also extend to some of the newer houses that have been built around the area. Shadowy figures are seen moving through the homes and residents have heard voices coming from empty rooms.

The Holy Cross is said to have become a very dangerous place, with a string of deaths having occurred there. It is reported that a gang with satanic beliefs actually sacrificed one of their own members in an attempt to call upon Satan to grant their wishes. Others say that a couple sought privacy within its walls and as a result of a quarrel, the man was killed, his body stuffed into a drain pipe.

Sheriffs patrol it often now and run people off who are in there and occasionally arrest them for trespassing.

Grant Corner Inn

122 Grant Avenue
Santa Fe, New Mexico

The Grant Corner Inn is located in a very elegant three story colonial style home built in 1905 for Judge Arthur Robinson and his wife for many, many years. It was then used as an office building in the 1950s and became an inn in 1982. It is located in the heart of downtown Santa Fe. The Inn proper contains nine rooms that are furnished with antiques. According to the literature on this charming little hotel, it prides itself on its friendly, warm atmosphere. What is seldom mentioned is that in addition to the charm and antique furnishings, is that this old home also comes with a few spirits.

THE GHOSTS

Custodians, guests, and visitors have reported a number of ghostly encounters over the years. Unexplainable sounds of heavy objects falling to the floor, doors banging shut, and loud footsteps are heard throughout the building. Police have been called on several occasions.

According to all reports, rooms 4 and 8 and the hallway on the second floor are the primary haunting sites. There have been incidents of the sounds of heavy objects falling on the floor, footsteps, and slamming doors. Later investigations reveal nothing has fallen and no explanation for the footsteps or slamming doors. Some witnesses have claimed to have seen a grayish figure in the hallways that always seems to vanish right before their eyes.

In "Adobe Angels: Ghosts of Santa Fe and Taos," Antonio Garcez interviewed Art Garcia, former caretaker of this B&B. Garcia's account was terrifying — he endured deafening noises, a blast of freezing air that killed his house plants, the stench of rotting meat. He tried to convince friends to stay with him, only to have them leave hurriedly, frightened for their lives.

According to owner Louise Stewart, the spirit that haunted her house so violently has since quieted down. Extensive remodeling has been done since Stewart bought the building ("We gutted it," she says), and she thinks the unhappy spirit may have left. Then again, maybe it's just waiting for the right guest to torment[7].

---

[7] Wheeler, Liza, N.M. Has Its Share of Haunts, Albuquerque Journal, Thursday, October 31, 2002.

LA Fonda Hotel

100 East San Francisco Street
Santa Fe, New Mexico

When Santa Fe was founded in 1607, official records show an inn or Fonda was among the first businesses established. More than two hundred years later, in 1821, when Captain William Becknell completed the first successful trading expedition from Missouri to Santa Fe - a route that came to be known as the Santa Fe Trail - he enjoyed the hospitality at the inn (la fonda), where the Santa Fe Trail terminated at the town's central Plaza.

The current La Fonda was built in 1922 on the site of the previous inns. In 1925 it was acquired by the Atchison, Topeka Santa Fe Railroad which leased it to Fred Harvey who operated it as one of his famous Harvey Houses. For more than 40 years, from 1926 to 1968, La Fonda was one of the more successful Harvey Houses, a renowned chain of fine hotels.

Since 1968, La Fonda has been locally owned and operated and has continued the same tradition of providing warm hospitality, excellent service and modern amenities while maintaining historic integrity and architectural authenticity.

Throughout its long history, La Fonda has changed and evolved many times, but it continues to be the true heart of Santa Fe for visitors and locals alike.

THE GHOSTS

The present La Plazuela Dining Room in this lovely old hotel was originally an enclosed courtyard that was situated around an old well. Over 100 years ago, during the period of time in which a casino operated in this historic old building, a salesman who had a streak of bad luck and lost all of his company's money left the gambling tables and leapt to his death into the old well. From time to time, guests in the dining room sometimes report seeing a man walk to the center of the room and then jump as if into an invisible hole and simply disappear.

This building is old — it was already built when the city of Santa Fe was founded in the early 1600s. Alan Jordan, president of About Walks and Tours in Santa Fe, says that at one point, court was held in the building, and the public hangings of those found guilty took place in the lobby.

Besides the hangings (as if they weren't enough), there were plenty of other documented deaths in the La Fonda. In 1867, when La Fonda was known as the "Exchange Hotel," building records show Judge John P. Slough was killed in the lobby by Captain Rynerson, a member of the Territorial Legislature representing Dona Ana County. Rynerson shot him in the stomach after Slough called him a liar and a thief. He was later acquitted. Many people believe the judge still haunts the building today.

The hotel archives also document the hanging death of some poor soul by a lynch mob in the hotel's back yard.[8]

---

[8] Ibid.

LA Residencia

820 Paseo De Peralta
Santa Fe, New Mexico

La Residencia, located at the corner of Palace Avenue and Paseo de Peralta is a long term nursing facility that has been operated by Presbyterian Medical Services since late in 1983. On October 14, 2003, the facility closed its doors for the final time. The move meant the 101 residents had to find new quarters within a short period of time and the 106 employees either had to look for new jobs or move into new quarters.

The facility that housed this nursing home was originally the site of the original St. Vincent Hospital, the Santa Fe community hospital.

THE GHOSTS

There are a number of former staff and, not a few residents, who talk of strange sounds coming from empty rooms as well as ghostly dark clad figures being glimpsed in the hallways at night. Others whisper of malevolent inhuman figures sticking their heads into rooms to glare at the terrified residents.

The muffled crying of a little boy who died in Room 311 when this as still the community hospital is still heard by nurses. The child and his father both died of injuries suffered in an automobile accident on Interstate 25. The eerie sounds from Room 311 are so frequent that the nursing home administrators try to keep the room unoccupied.

The hauntings of the upper floors seemed to be taken in stride by the nursing staff. However, almost all of them wanted nothing to do with the basement of the building. The staff was almost unanimous in their belief that something evil lurked in the darkened corridors of the bottom floor.

When the State Museum, which is located in the building next door, began storing Indian artifacts in part of the huge basement, some nurses absolutely refused to enter the area. Those that would speak of their experiences claimed that they saw shadowy figures moving about the hallways and heard strange sounds such as banging and voices talking rapidly emanate from the basement rooms.

As usually happens in every organization the old timers thought it was fun to require the newcomers to the staff to go through a "rite of passage" that required them to spend some time in the basement. One of the staff members would take the new employee to the basement on the elevator and then required the rookie to cross the darkened basement to the stairway and then ascend to the third floor.

However one evening, a new staff member, a very young, inexperienced, nurse's aide, was taken to the basement and given her assignment. The one that had taken her to the basement then returned to the third floor to await the rookie's arrival. Traditionally, the newcomer always arrived shortly with some truly bizarre stories of thinks in the dark. This time, the new staff member did not arrive via the stairs; in fact, she did not arrive at all.

Concerned that something had happened to the young girl, two nurses went to the dark basement to look for the nurse's aide. They searched the main part of the basement, but found no sign of the aide. Finally, in desperation, they begin to call her name. Finally, she answered, her voice faint and far away. With the aid of a flashlight, the two nurses finally located the newcomer, in a small dark room, far down one of the hallways, crouched in the corner.

The very scared young lady confessed that she had become disoriented in the dark and lost her way. When she heard something moving in the darkness, she had run until she found the small room in which she was hiding. The older nurse calmed the young aide and the two started for the door. Then they both froze – oozing down the wall beside the doorway of the small room was fresh blood. The nurse later said that it covered most of the wall and seemed to actually be coming from then wall. Not waiting to see anything else, the two ran for the elevator where the other nurse was holding the car.

Later, the nurses discovered that St. Vincent's had once had a small incinerator in that same room where hospital maintenance personnel had cremated amputated limbs.

Penitentiary of New Mexico, Santa Fe

P.O. Box 1059
Santa Fe, New Mexico

The Main Unit of the Penitentiary of New Mexico at Santa Fe was opened in 1956 to house long term offenders. In 1980, there was a major rebellion at the New Mexico State Penitentiary, though it was said to have been an inmate rebellion without a plan, without leadership and without goals. Once the uprising began, a sort of mob mentality seemed to overcome the rioting inmates. There were few heroes, plenty of villains and many victims.

When State Police marched into the Penitentiary of New Mexico on Feb. 3, 1980, they didn't retake the prison from rioting inmates so much as they occupied the charred shell after the riot had burned itself out.

Thirty-three inmates were found dead inside -- some of them horribly butchered by their fellow prisoners. The emergency room at St. Vincent Hospital in Santa Fe was overwhelmed with more than 100 inmates -- some beaten, others suffering from drug overdoses. Eight of the 12 guards who had been taken hostage were treated for injuries, though, amazingly, none of the guards had been killed. It was a black mark on New Mexico history as the nation was captivated by the horror stories that dribbled out of Santa Fe.

The riot began in the early morning hours of Saturday, Feb. 2, when guards entered dormitory E-2 on the south side of the prison.

For some unknown reason, the door to the dormitory wasn't locked, in violation of prison security procedures. Neither was a hallway gate that led to the prison control room. Four guards were taken hostage during the first few minutes of the riot. In all, there were 15 guards on duty inside the prison that night, supervising more than 1,100 inmates.

Inmates rushed down the main corridor and broke the shatterproof glass at the control center. The guard on duty fled, leaving behind keys that could open most of the prison gates and doors.

Once the inmates assumed control of the cellblocks, the inside of the prison became a nightmare of violence. One Associated Press reporter later described it in a story distributed worldwide as a "merry-go-round gone crazy." A large number of fires were set as other inmates ripped out plumbing fixtures, flooding parts of the prison. Other inmates got into the infirmary and began taking drugs while still others began hunting their enemies and found them.

Sometime around 8 a.m. that Saturday morning, inmates began using tools from the prison to gain access to cellblock 4, which housed the "snitches" and inmates in protective segregation. The "snitches" housed in that cellblock all met a horrible end. One was hung from the upper tier of the cellblock, another decapitated. Most of the 33 inmates killed were from the segregation unit.

Early Saturday morning, fitful negotiations began with some inmate leaders. Ambulances shuttled the dead and injured to St. Vincent Hospital in Santa Fe. Smoke continued to pour out of the prison gymnasium.

It became clear later that neither the inmates nor the state had a single spokesman during the negotiations. This resulted in a great deal of confusion in the attempted negotiations. Eventually, however, the prison inmates made 11 basic demands. Some concerned basic prison conditions like overcrowding, inmate discipline, educational services and improving food. They also wanted outside witnesses to the negotiations such as federal officials and the news media.

Guards who had been taken hostage when the riot started were finally released. Some of the guards had been protected by inmates; others were brutally beaten. "One was tied to a chair. Another lay naked on a stretcher, blood pouring from a head wound," a Journal reporter wrote. Negotiations broke off about 1 a.m. Sunday and state officials insisted no concessions had been made. But the riot, fueled by drugs and hate, was running out of gas.

Later Sunday morning, inmates began to trickle out of the prison, seeking refuge at the fence where National Guardsmen stood with their M-16s. Black inmates led the exodus from the smoldering cellblocks, staying in groups large enough to defend themselves from other inmates. The largest riot in New Mexico Prison History was over.

THE GHOSTS

Many have said that violent emotion can produce hauntings and this prison riot released emotions that had been suppressed for years. Inmates went on a killing spree unprecedented in New Mexico prison history.

The most active areas of the prison are Cell Blocks 3, 4, the Tool room and the laundry room. Cell Block 3 was the maximum security ward which also contained the Solitary confinement cell. Some of the ghostly activity reported here includes unexplainable noises, doors that open and close by themselves, and lights that turn on and off without any apparent cause.

Cell block 4 was the area where the "snitches" and other prisoners held in protective custody were contained. Upon entering the cell block, there are marks on the floor where rioters used power tools to decapitate the snitches and several other inmates. Also visible are the outlines of scorch marks where other inmates were burned to death with propane cutting torches. Another inmate was hung from the upper tier of the cell block with sheets that had been tied together. The activity reported here is similar to those reported in Cell Block 3. Twenty three of the inmates that were murdered during the riot were killed in Cell Block 4.

The laundry was the site of several murders, although they occurred long before the riot of 1980. It is located in a labyrinth of corridors that lie underneath the prison. These corridors also link to the gas chamber, many mechanical rooms and the tool room where the inmates stole the propane torches and other tools that were used during the riots. Uneasy feelings and whispers are often reported down there as well as unusual human shaped shadows.

Dripping Springs

Las Cruces, New Mexico

Dripping Springs has long been an area enveloped in mystery. Col. Eugene Van Patten originally built the Dripping Springs Resort in the 1870's. A native of New York State, Van Patten came to Mesilla at the invitation of his uncle, John Butterfield, who operated the Butterfield Stage Line. Van Patten worked at the Picacho Stage Station and probably elsewhere after the stage line ceased operations in the Las Cruces area in 1861. During the Civil War he joined the Confederacy and saw action in the Battle of Glorietta Pass near Santa Fe.

Dripping Springs Resort was originally called "Van Patten's Mountain Camp." It had approximately 16 rooms, a large dining room and a concert hall. It was very popular around the turn of the century and many famous people, including Pat Garret and Pancho Villa, have stayed there. Van Patten was married to a local Piro Indian woman and a number of Indians lived and worked at the resort. The Indians hand-carried water from the spring to the rooms in "ollas" attached to long wooden poles and, from time to time, held dances for the amusement of the guests.

In the late 1800's a stage line brought guests to the hotel from Las Cruces, 17 miles away. The stage would deliver the guests to the front of the hotel and then return to the livery. The wagons and horses for the stage line, as well as the personal livestock of the guests were kept in this area. In the 1900's guests began to arrive by automobile as well as by horse and wagon.

The resort had its share of exciting times. When Albert J. Fountain, a prominent figure in the Lincoln County War, was murdered on the East Side of the Organ Mountains in 1896, his daughter was notified of the murder at the resort. Van Patten led a large posse to investigate but Fountain's body, and that of his 12-year-old son Henry, were never found.

In 1917 Van Patten went bankrupt and Dripping Springs was sold to Dr. Nathan Boyd who homesteaded on a parcel of land adjacent to the resort. Boyd was a physician in San Francisco who later married the daughter of a wealthy Australian engineer. Boyd joined his in-laws' business and became involved in large engineering projects all over the world. He and his wife came to Las Cruces to promote, design and build a dam on the Rio Grande whose floods often devastated the countryside. Local farmers whose lands would have been inundated by the lake behind the dam stopped the dam. Ironically, the U.S. Bureau of Reclamation, creating the state's largest man-made lake, Elephant Butte Reservoir, eventually built a dam farther north. By the time Boyd had acquired Van Patten's resort, his wife had contracted tuberculosis. Deciding to remain in Las Cruces, Boyd converted Dripping Springs into a sanitarium. New structures were built in different parts of the canyon to provide housing and care for the patients.

The Boyd family eventually sold the property to another physician, a Dr. Sexton of Las Cruces, who continued to operate it as a sanatorium. As late as 1946 the resort was still in relatively good shape and a group of local citizens attempted to raise $4,000 to purchase it for historic preservation. Unfortunately, their effort failed and unknown persons scavenged the resort for building materials.

Today, the ruins of Dripping Springs Resort lie scattered along the canyon, preserving the memory of Col. Van Patten, the doctors Boyd and Sexton, and the many famous and not so famous who visited there.

THE GHOSTS

The complex that was once known as Boyd's Sanatorium sits silently, brooding over the deserted canyons, still mostly hidden from view behind clusters of rocky outcroppings and pockets of thick, thorny desert fauna. These buildings, which were once all part of a tuberculosis sanatorium, were constructed around 1910 by Dr. Nathan Boyd, medical doctor and international businessman. Legend says that Dr. Boyd had a beloved wife who was suffering from the terrible disease, and that he built the place, up in the rugged yet beautiful mountains, for her.

There are other, darker, rumors about Boyd's Sanatorium, as well. Rumors of a more... unknown element. Some say that this canyon is filled with restless spirits, and that some of them happen to be the spirits of the patients who passed away up at the mountainside sanatorium.

The deserted building known as the Caretaker's house had a wooden porch with a breath-taking view of the valley below. It is not hard to imagine that there might be spirits here. The trail leading up to this place is officially closed every day well before dark, earlier in fact than all of the other trails in the area. And, there have been reports of campers in the nearby canyon campgrounds being terrified by strange visions and horrific nightmares featuring torturous treatments undergone by gaunt and ghostly "patients," even though some of the campers are said to have no prior knowledge of the nearby sanatorium's presence.

There have been various paranormal investigations at this location; one group even claims to have gotten photos of "shadowy figures" in the ruins. In fact, it was here at Boyd's Sanatorium where a number of new cameras failed to work. In each case, the camera had worked fine at the Van Patten ruins, and it began to work once again as soon as the would be photographer went a little ways down the trail away from the sanatorium... it just would not function while in the vicinity of the sanatorium.

A hand-hewn stone stairway heads up the mountainside to where the patients housing used to stand. All that remains of these buildings now are the foundations and low stone walls that outline the shapes of where they once existed. On this pathway can be found the remains of an old drinking fountain designed to aid those who took this way up the canyon. Water was piped in from the springs nearby to a holding tank above the terraces where the patient's housing stood; piping carried the water down to the residences and the drinking fountain below. The kitchen and dining hall was located in a separate structure, perched high atop stilt-like beams along the mountainside.

In the early 1900's, Dr. Boyd was involved in a court case that would eventually deplete his funds; the sanatorium was sold to a Dr. T.C. Sexton from Las Cruces in the 1920's. It was intermittently run as a sanatorium and resort for several more years. Nathan Boyd's son, Earl, bought the place back in the early 1930's and moved onto the land, living in the Caretaker's house. In 1940, while Earl Boyd was away serving in the military, the remote structures were subjected to heavily damaging vandalism and looting by unknown parties. The place has been vacant ever since, despite changing hands one more time before being acquired by the Bureau of Land Management in 1988.

In spite of Federal government ownership, there are still figures that are seen moving about in the shadows as evening falls. Locals still say do not be caught around the Sanitarium after dark.

Montezuma's Castle

Montezuma, New Mexico.

Montezuma's Castle, originally known as the Montezuma Hotel, was designed by noted Chicago architects John Root and Daniel Burnham for the Atchison, Topeka & Santa Fe Railroad, which had built a spur from nearby Las Vegas, NM to Montezuma in 1882. For a decade, the resort was a major attraction and visitors included Rutherford B. Hayes, Ulysses S. Grant, William Tecumseh Sherman and Theodore Roosevelt before the Montezuma closed as a hotel in 1903.

The Castle was later owned by the Baptist Church and served as the site of its Montezuma College and then by the Catholic Church which ran a seminary for Mexican priests from 1937-1972. Once the Catholic Church closed the seminary, the Castle was left empty and became easy prey for a decade of vandalism. In 1981, the Armand Hammer Foundation bought the property in order to found the United States campus of the United World Colleges.

The Castle remained an empty but picturesque backdrop to the UWC-USA campus until 1997 when it garnered national attention. First, the National Trust for Historic Preservation recognized the building as one of America's most endangered historic places. In 1998, the White House Millennium Council named it one of “America’s Treasures”, the first property west of the Mississippi to receive that honor.

In 1998, the UWC-USA launched its first capital campaign, Save the Castle-Serve the World, raising funds for scholarship endowments, program development, campus improvements and the restoration of the Montezuma Castle.

In 2000-2001, the building underwent a $10.5 million renovation, transforming it into an international center with student and faculty housing, dining facilities, offices, a campus store and student social center. The Castle also holds the Bartos Institute for the Constructive Engagement of Conflict.

While many of the building’s magnificent interior and exterior details were restored, modern treasures were added, including two eight-foot glass sculptures designed specifically for the Castle’s enormous dining room by artist Dale Chihuly.

THE GHOSTS

A large number of people have reported seeing the figure of a woman in one of the towers at night. She seems to be watching for something or someone. Others have reported hearing strange sounds coming from some of the empty rooms of this massive structure. There have also been voices heard when there was no one around the account for them.

EL Rancho Hotel

Gallup, NM

Formally opened December 17, 1937, The EL Rancho Hotel was built by the brother of the movie magnet, D.W. Griffith. Drawn by the many films made in the area, Ronald Reagan, Spencer Tracy, Katherine Hepburn and Kirk Douglas were among the many stars listed in the guest register. Autographed photos of the stars, Navajo Rugs & Mounted trophy animal heads adorn the magnificent two story open lobby with its circular staircase.

The El Rancho Hotel was built by Joe Massaglia in 1937 for R.E. "Griff" Griffith. Originally, Griffith came to Gallup to direct a film. He later returned to build the El Rancho Hotel. He also managed the local Chief Theater. From the 1930's to 1950's, the hotel became a temporary home for many Hollywood stars. It also became a stopping point for tourists driving on old Route 66. The hotel is now protected by the National Historic Preservation Society. This historic hotel is continually cared for by Mr. Ortega who has made it his personal hobby since its purchase.

The hotel is decorated and furnished in the Old West rustic style. It is constructed of original brick, ash tar stone, and huge wooden beams with a pitched wood shale roof. The large portico overlooks the entrance and reflects the Southern Plantation style. Entering through the solid wood doors, one views the grandeur of the lobby. The floor is brick, inlaid in a basket weave pattern, and the light fixtures are made of stamped aluminum. The stone fireplace cove is surrounded by handmade wooden staircases that spiral to the second floor balcony. The balcony encircles the lobby and displays original photos of the hotel and many autographed pictures of the Hollywood stars. Mr. Armand Ortega has recaptured the hotel's splendor and charm of yesterday.

A large number of Hollywood's most famous movies were shot in the area such as :The Bad Man, an MGM film starring Wallace Beery & Ronald Reagan in 1940; Sundown, a Wanger film starring Gene Tierney in 1941; Desert Song, starring Dennis Morgan in 1942; Song Of The Nile, starring Maria Montez & Jon Hall in 1944; Four Faces West & Colorado Territory, both starring Joel McCrea in 1947-48; Streets Of Laredo, starring William Holden & William Bendix in 1948; Rocky Mountain, starring Errol Flynn in 1950; Big Carnival, starring Kirk

Douglas in 1950; Raton Pass, starring Dennis Morgan in 1951; New Mexico, starring Lew Ayres in 1950; Fort Defiance, starring Dane Clark in 1950; Fort Massacre, starring Joel McCrea in 1957; A Distant Trumpet, starring Troy Donahue & Suzanne Pleshette in 1963; The Hallelujah Trail, starring Burt Lancaster & Lee Remick in 1964.

THE GHOSTS

A number of guests as well as staff members have reported hearing disembodied footsteps and laughter on the upper floor of the lobby after hours.

Objects have been reported to have been moved about throughout various locations of the hotel by unseen hands. The mysterious opening and closing of doors has been reported in the bridal suite.

Econo Lodge, Grants

1509 E. Santa Fe Avenue
Grants, New Mexico

The Econo Lodge in Grants, New Mexico is an older three story hotel. Though no one seems to be completely certain of how it happened, this hotel has gained a certain reputation for being a very haunted place to stay.

I am told that though there are three floors to the facility, no one is allowed on the third floor. All of the rooms on that level are now used for storage. However,

Figure 11: The Econo Lodge in Grants, New Mexico.

even though no one is ever allowed to be on that floor, from the swimming pool, many people have seen people looking down at them from the third floor.

A number of guests have reported hearing footsteps, the sounds of screams and the distinctive sounds of elevators going to that level. These same people have also said that when they inquired, it is revealed that the elevators do not go to the third floor. It takes a key for the elevator to go past the second floor.

Former staff members have said that they have heard that an unknown person appears in the kitchen out of nowhere. Whenever this figure mysteriously appears in the kitchen, the entire room becomes as cold as an icebox.

Other people have said that all of the stories about the hotel being haunted are fake and it started as a joke. Some have tried to confirm the incidents that have led to the hauntings, but can find no newspaper stories about the deaths. When asked, some of the local people submit that the town covered up the murders in order to not scare away tourists.

According to the story told by those who confirm that the hotel is haunted, there was a rather attractive young lady who worked as a hotel maid. She had been called to bring some towels to a guest staying on the third floor.

When she arrived, however, he pulled her into the room, raped and murdered her.

Some of the staff who claim to have actually gotten to the third floor to investigate the story claim that the yellow police barrier tape is still in place on the left wing of the third floor. These same staff members also report that if you actually get to the room and enter it, that it is possible to still smell the blood and they are all adamant that the room is very cold.

According to the locals, the third floor was closed off because other guests were reported that at midnight they could hear screams of terror coming from that room and the sounds of a struggle. There are also some reports that this was not the only murder to take place on the third floor of the Econo Lodge in Grants. Some people say that the hotel is filled with evil that tends to cause the violence. Finally, there are a number of reports that if you stay on the second floor in the room directly beneath the murder room, that during the night you will hear screaming and cries for help coming from the room above.

Pendaries Restaurant & Lodge

Pendaries Village
Rociada, New Mexico

Pendaries is a subdivision located in Rociada, New Mexico (about 30 miles northwest of Las Vegas). The main attractions include the 18 hole mountain golf course, fishing, hiking and just plain old relaxation. The subdivision has roughly 980 original lots in the subdivision. Of the original lots, approximately 100 are on the market for resale purposes. The Rociada valley and surrounding communities hold a fascinating history and several buildings constructed in the 1870's can still be seen today.

The Lodge has 18 rooms that have been freshly painted and have new carpeting. Roll-a-way beds for families are available. There are also additional accommodations available in summer homes. The full-service restaurant serves dinner daily. Breakfast and lunch may be enjoyed at the Club House near the Golf Shop. Enjoy a drink in the historic Moosehead Saloon. The Conference Center seats 80 for meetings and is also available for banquets. The restaurant, seating 100, provides the opportunity for banquets of larger groups.

Pendaries Village was established in the mid 1960's and this little subdivision has grown into a unique opportunity for outdoor enthusiasts to live and/or vacation. Just 2 hours from Albuquerque this is the perfect weekend getaway. Home to over 190 residences and a challenging 18 hole mountain golf course. You will find plenty of time (and privacy) for hiking, fishing, mountain biking and golfing.

THE GHOSTS

Many of the employees have seen an older man in the downstairs bar. No one knows his identity, but this mysterious figure will suddenly be seen standing by the bar and then he will vanish. This mysterious figure had also been seen standing outside one of the rooms in the lodge as if waiting for someone.

Philmont Scount Camp

Philmont, New Mexico

Philmont Scout Ranch is the oldest of the "high-adventure bases" operated by the Boy Scouts of America, along with the Florida High Adventure Sea Base and a collection of programs in the Boundary Waters. It is one of the most renowned BSA facilities[9].

Philmont is located in the Sangre de Cristo Range of the Rocky Mountains of New Mexico. The closest town is Cimarron, New Mexico, but perhaps it is better to say that it is about 20 miles west-northwest of Springer, New Mexico, or 35 miles southwest of Raton, New Mexico. It is shaped somewhat like the letter 'I,' with the bottom section larger than the top. It is about 12 miles across (east to west) at its widest point, and about 30 miles long. There are no mountains to the south of Philmont, or to the east (indeed, part of the eastern fringe of the ranch is flatland) but the interior is quite mountainous.

---

[9] http://en.wikipedia.org/wiki/Philmont_Scout_Ranch

The lowest elevation is 6500 feet, at the southeast corner. The highest point is the peak of Baldy Mountain (12,441 feet), on the northwest boundary. The most recognizable landmark at Philmont is the Tooth of Time (9003 feet), a granite monolith protruding 500 vertical feet from an east-west ridge. Tooth of Time Ridge, and the latitude line it sits on, marks the boundary between the central and southern sections of Philmont. The boundary between the central and northern sections is the narrowest part of the 'I'-shape, only a few miles across. U.S. Highway 64 runs through Philmont just south of this line.

Native Americans of the Jicarrilla Apache tribe and Ute tribe once inhabited Philmont. At least one Native American archaeological site exists in the northern section, and various camps seek to preserve Philmont's Native American heritage. In the mid-19th century, the Santa Fe Trail crossed the plains just southwest of Philmont. The Tooth of Time owes its name to this trail; travelers knew that once they passed it, they had only a few weeks to go until they reached Santa Fe, New Mexico. Philmont's strategic location along the trail spurred some interest in it. In 1841, Carlos Beaubien and Guadalupe Miranda obtained a large land grant from the Mexican government, including the present ranch. Soon the grant fell into the hands of

Beaubien's son-in-law Lucien Maxwell, who played an important role in developing and settling it. Maxwell sold the ranch to the Maxwell Land Grant and Railroad Company, which gave up and handed it on to a Dutch development company, which decided to parcel it out to ranchers.

An old Mexican homestead was preserved on the ranch, as part of Abreu camp, for many years until it burned down, leaving only a stone fireplace and chimney. A reconstructed homestead may be seen less than a mile away at New Abreu camp. Herds of cattle, another relic of this era, graze in the numerous meadows of southeastern Philmont.

The history of mining at Philmont dates back to the years immediately after the Civil War. The story is that an Indian befriended a Union soldier, and happened to give him a shiny rock. (This contributor finds the story suspect, because any Union troops stationed in New Mexico at the time would have been involved in driving out the Native Americans.) The shiny material in the rock was found to be copper. According to the story, the soldier and two of his friends went up to investigate, and found gold. However, they could not stay and mine the gold, and by the time they returned the next year, the area was overrun by miners.

Scores of gold mines were excavated in Philmont, and operated into the early 20th century. A large vein of gold is said to lie under Baldy Mountain to this day, but extracting it has not been feasible. The Contention Mine, located at Cyphers Mine camp, is open to guided tours.

The penultimate owner of Philmont was wealthy oil magnate and wilderness enthusiast Waite Phillips, who amassed a large part of the old land grant in the 1920s. Phillips built a large residence at Philmont, and called it the Villa Philmonte. He also constructed a number of hunting lodges and day-use camps. It would not have been beyond his means to bring electricity to those camps, but he decided not to. Some of these camps have been preserved, complete with wood-burning stoves, oil lamps, and other design features indicative of Phillips's often eccentric taste. (This particular contributor personally saw two of these preserved facilities, at the camps known as Fish Camp and Hunting Lodge.) Phillips used the ranch as a private game reserve, but would sometimes allow others to use it, including a few Boy Scout troops. He was so impressed with the Scouts that in 1938, he donated a significant part of it to the Boy Scouts of America. They initially named it the "Philturn Rockymountain Scoutcamp" [sic]. The word 'Philturn' comes from Waite Phillips's name, together with the

"Good Turn" he did by donating the property. In 1941, Phillips added the rest of the present Philmont property, including the Villa Philmonte. To help fund the upkeep of Philmont, he threw in a large office building in Tulsa, Oklahoma. The ranch's name was changed at this time.

Philmont was run differently in the early years than it is now. Half a dozen "base camps" were constructed at strategic locations. A visiting group of Scouts would stay at one of these camps for a week, and day-hike to surrounding locations of interest. (Conventional stationary camps are usually operated in this manner, as well.) If the Scouts wanted to visit a different area, they would pack up their gear, hoist it onto donkeys, and hike to another base camp. Eventually, possibly due to the advent of modern lightweight metal-frame backpacks and other backpacking technology, the program was restructured to be backpacking-based.

Most of those who come to Philmont come for the trek, an 11-day backpacking trip. (A group of Scouts on a trek is called a crew.) Other program options include:

Cavalcades are similar to standard treks, but conducted on horseback.

Rayado Treks are twice as long as standard treks, and considerably more strenuous. Rayado crews are put together by Philmont staff, and consist of people from different parts of the country.

The Philmont Training Center offers weeklong training programs for adult leaders, and a variety of outdoor programs for trainees' families.

The Roving Outdoor Conservation School and various Trail Crew programs teach participants about ecology, conservation techniques, and trail construction methods.

Guided activities such as fishing, winter camping, and skiing, are offered throughout the year.

The area known as Base Camp is a town unto itself. It has a post office, half a dozen chapels (operating daily), two dining halls, a clinic, a store for souvenirs and sundry camping gear, housing (mainly tents) for roughly 900 staff, and tents for between 800 and 1000 trekkers. Trekkers are organized into crews of seven to twelve (usually closer to twelve than to seven), with two to four adult leaders. A contingent consists of one or more crews from the same council (see Boy Scouts of America: Organization), traveling together. Around 360 trekkers arrive at Base Camp every day of the season. When they arrive, they are assigned a ranger, a young man or woman highly skilled in backpacking. The ranger's task is to guide the crew through "processing," (basically, registration), to make sure that the trekkers actually know how to backpack, and to teach them Philmont-specific camping practices.

Crews are required to pick up a dining fly. This is a 12-foot-square tarp with two collapsible aluminum poles. Its purpose (quite contrary to the name) is to serve as a rain cover for the crew's backpacks. It is supposed to be set up as an A-frame, with two opposite sides staked down, the middle held up by the poles, and the ends open. Many crews experiment with the use of trees, hiking poles, and other devices to obtain a roomier configuration so that it can be used for crew activities such as card games. Crews may also pick up Philmont tents. These tents are also A-frame, five feet wide by seven feet long, with a rain fly. They are more difficult to set up than conventional dome tents, but very easy to break down. They have a bad reputation, which this contributor considers to be undeserved, since they are not significantly heavier than commonly used dome tents.

Crews also pick up several days' worth of Philmont food (see "Commissaries" below). Philmont also provides optional cooking supplies.

After processing, crews are loaded up onto busses and shipped off to any of several trailheads, called "turnarounds" because there is a loop in the road for the bus to turn around. The crew and its ranger are now alone.

THE GHOSTS

Having now mentioned most of the information that can be found in the literature about this Scout Camp, let us now turn our attention to those things that are only whispered about after the lights go out. It seems that the Philmont Scout Camp is also haunted.

One of the ghosts that has been seen, in addition to the spirit of the Shaman that haunts Urraca Mesa, has been that of Thomas “Black Jack” Ketchum, the only person ever hanged in Clayton, New Mexico. He was also the only man ever hanged for train robbery in the entire state, a law that was later found to be unconstitutional. But, unfortunately, this determination was a little too late for poor Black Jack.

There is a story told by a former scout about his meeting with Black Jack Ketchum while camping on the Philmont Scout Camp. He and several other scouts were backpacking through the mountains, visiting various historic sites, including an abandoned gold mine, a ghost town and one of Black Jack Ketchum's outlaw hideouts.

The outlaw hideout was a large rock overhang and the scouts thought it would be fun to camp there for the night. However, their leader insisted that they stay at a nearby-designated site. Disappointed at being refused the opportunity for they thought would be an exciting time, several of the scouts set their tents up several hundred feet away from the leader's tent, hoping they would have a chance to sneak back to the hideout later that night.

About 11:00 p.m., when the rest of the camp was fast asleep, five of the scouts gathered their sleeping bags and quietly stole back to the hideout. They set up camp under the overhang and built a fire, where they sat around talking about their trip. When the fire burned down to nothing more than red coals, the scouts settled down in their sleeping bags. The storyteller drifted off to sleep thinking about Black Jack. Suddenly, he was awakened by a noise in the bushes. He said that he felt paralyzed, unable to move and tried to call out to the others, but his throat was all knotted up.

Then he saw a cowboy, dressed all in black come running out of the bushes toward the hide out. He said the man was mostly solid but some parts of him appeared translucent. He described the man as filthy dirty, with a tattered hat, clothes from the 1800's, and terribly yellowed teeth. His face was very red, glistening with sweat, with lots of facial hair and the apparition held a revolver.

The cowboy was apparently unaware of the scout, but the boy was very scared, as much by his inability to move than by the man. As he watched, a strange fog emanated from the tree line across from a small stream and he could hear men yelling unintelligently, and then muffled gunfire.

The cowboy turned and fired his revolver six times into the trees and then ran and stood right over the scout. The cowboy was wounded in the shoulder and as he reloaded his pistol, he discharged six shell casings from his revolver that fell right on top of the boy. As the scout watched in amazement, the casings disappeared as they fell onto his sleeping bag. The cowboy then finished reloading his revolver and fired additional shots into the trees.

Suddenly, the cowboy seemed to become aware of the young scout. The expression on the cowboy's face indicated that the scout had just suddenly appeared before his eyes. The cowboy seemed to be confused and confounded, while the scout was just simply terrified. Then, the cowboy un-cocked and lowered his pistol, looked at the scout very closely, and said, "You're not supposed to be here," and then just disappeared into thin air.

Eventually, he was able to go back to sleep, but had to be shaken repeatedly by his fellow campers before waking in the morning. As the scouts broke camp, the boy told his fellow campers about the "dream," who were amused by the story. But, as the scout rolled up his sleeping bag, he found six shell casings in the dust.

Later, when they returned to base camp, the scout visited an old saloon, where a photograph of Black Jack Ketchum was displayed. The photograph was the same man that the scout had seen at the hideout.

When he told his friends, they brushed him off, as setting them up for a big hoax and the scout never told anyone about it again, but he kept the shell casings. After the scout returned home, he checked with a gun expert who said the casings were dated from sometime around 1878, but were in almost brand new condition and the gunpowder could still be smelt in them. In fact, the gunpowder was one that was used in the last century, but not today.

The scout kept the shell casings for years, but unfortunately, after he moved away from home, his mother threw them out along with several other items the boy had saved, such as comic books and baseball cards.

New Mexico Military Institute

101 West College Boulevard
Roswell, New Mexico

The New Mexico Military Institute was established in 1891 and became a State (Territorial) School in 1893. Its purpose then and now is "for the education and training of the youth of this country with a mandate by law to be of as high a standard as like institutions in other states and territories of the United States."

New Mexico Military Institute is primarily an academic institution operating within the framework of a military environment. However, in spite of the fact that it is a school that prides itself on looking to the future, it must still deal with some holdovers from the past.

THE GHOSTS

The New Mexico Military Institute does not use the phonetic alphabet 'J' for Juliet for one of its troops for a very simple reason...it is believed to be cursed. Back in the 1800's when the school was still an all male military school in the frontier Juliet troop was on of the troops to go out and defend the school from Indians and other wild west characters. After one such excursion, no one from the Juliet troop survived.

Former students have reported that a tower with a clock was built in their honor and the letter 'J' has not been used as a unit designation since that time. However, to add another interesting dimension to this school, it is said that on some days when the sun is just right if you look up at the tower you can see faces in the rock of the boys who lost their lives defending their school looking back down at you.

I have also heard stories about shadowy figures being seen moving across the parade grounds in the early hours of the morning. There have also been stories told by former students about strange sounds and voices being heard in empty rooms.

Eagles Nest, New Mexico

Eagles Nest is located in the Moreno Valley in the midst of the beautiful Sangre de Cristo Mountains. Nestled between the states two highest peaks - Baldy Mountain (12,441 feet) and Wheeler Peek (13,161 feet), it sits at the junction of US Hwy 64 and State Hwy 38. High above sea level, at 8,300 feet, the village rests on the western slope of Baldy Mountain, an area rich in Gold Rush history.

Before the miners, the area was called home by the Ute and Jicarrilla Apache Indians who roamed the area in search of game and golden feathers for ceremonial worship. When Elizabethtown, just 5 and 1/2 miles north, was in its heyday, the Eagle Nest area was utilized mostly for ranching and farming.

In 1873 Charles and Frank Springer founded the CS Ranch on the banks of the Cimarron River and in 1907 they applied for a permit to build the Eagle Nest Dam. It was almost 10 years before the Springers could hire the engineering firm of Bartlett and Ranney of San Antonio, Texas to design and build the dam. Finally, in 1916 construction on the dam was begun and was completed in 1918 to store the surplus waters of the Cimarron River for power plants, mining and irrigation. Most of the labor for building the dam was provided by the Taos Pueblo Indians. The largest privately constructed dam in the United States, the concrete structure is 400 feet wide, stands 140 feet above the river bed, and is 9.5 feet thick at its crest and 45.2 feet thick at its base. Supposedly, eagles built nests on the sides of the new dam and that's how it got its name.

The Eagle Nest Dam, completed in 1918, is the largest privately constructed dam in the United States. The dam created the Eagle Nest Lake which varies between 1,500 and 3,000 surface acres, depending upon weather cycles. Surrounded by rolling pasture and stunning mountains, the fishermen began to arrive when the lake was stocked with trout. Along with the fishermen, entrepreneurs also arrived, building businesses and transforming the quiet farming community into a tourist mecca, providing entertainment to the visiting cowboys, fishermen and other tourists.

One of the biggest industries was cutting and selling ice from the lake. T.D. Neal hired men to drive out upon the lake and cut block ice that was stored in ice houses filled with sawdust. Jobs were scarce in the area and many families survived the winters by ice cutting and trapping.

In the 1920's illegal gambling was introduced to the area. Eagle Nest became a popular spot along the road from Santa Fe to Raton where politicians and other travelers attended the horse races. A favorite stop over for the dignitaries, they were said to have caused quite a ruckus with their gambling, drinking and dancing.

In 1927, Walter Gant, an oilman from Oklahoma hired a business man by the name of William B. Tyer to oversee the construction of the grandest resort that Eagle Nest had ever seen -- the Eagle Nest Lodge. Bill Tyer lived in a cabin on the Gant property and oversaw the many details of building the luxurious lodge. When it was completed, Bill Tyer stayed on to manage the Eagle Nest Lodge, which featured 12 rooms, a lounge, a restaurant, horseback riding, fishing, and hunting expeditions for the many travelers who stopped to enjoy its magnificent view of Eagle Nest Lake. Considered the finest lodge for miles, it soon expanded to include a guest annex that featured five studio units with their own bathrooms and kitchenettes. They also connected the main building to the Casa Loma via a walkway/lounge they called the Loafer's Lounge.

The local saloons heartedly welcomed the travelers, rolling slot machines out upon the boardwalk early in the morning to entice the gamblers. Judge Neblett, for whom the Colin Neblett Wildlife Area is named, was a frequent visitor, as well as several governors. Though gambling was illegal, it was obviously overlooked by the politicians. In fact, it has been said by several of the locals, that when illegal gambling was first introduced to Eagle Nest in the 1920s, that the local Sheriff owned many of the slot machines in Eagle Nest, Red River and Colfax County. However, since we first published this story in the summer of 2003, we have since heard from Jerry Ficklin, a local historian and writer, who once lived in Eagle Nest and spent many summers there between the years of 1945 and 1960, that this "tidbit" is nothing more than a legend with no documented support.

The El Monte Hotel (now the Laguna Vista), as well as Doughbelly's Cafe (now the building that houses Julio's,) The Gold Pan, and the Eagle Nest Lodge offered roulette and gaming tables, as well as slot machines. Slot machines were also found in many of the stores.

Eagle Nest was in its heyday during the 1930's, with disputes often resulting in shots fired back and forth across Main Street. Reportedly one saloon owner, along the road that travels north from Eagle Nest to Idlewild, was known to provide free wine to those who came through its doors. The free pouring wine would inevitably lead to fights and discord among the rowdy customers, which the saloon "advertised" as free entertainment.

The Laguna Vista Saloon

Eagles Nest, New Mexico

Locals call the Laguna Vista Saloon, built in 1898, the "Guney". The El Monte, as it was originally called, was allegedly built with stolen railroad ties, which are still visible in some of the rooms. A would-be innkeeper transported the petrified railroad ties from Ute Park to Elizabethtown for two summers, but when he returned after the winter, the railroad ties were missing and a new hotel had been built in Therma, which later changed its name to Eagle Nest. Behind the original saloon were a 17-foot deep hand dug well and several icehouses.

The El Monte was one of the busiest saloons in the 1920's and 30's when the politicians stopped over on their way to the horse races in Raton, New Mexico to partake of the many roulette, gaming tables and slot machines offered in the saloons, inns, and businesses of Eagle Nest. It was sometime during this period that the El Monte's name was changed to the Laguna Vista Lodge and was operated by a couple named Gene and Pearl Wilson. At this time, the Wilsons often had to protect their gambling profits when transporting them from the saloon to their living quarters, by arming themselves with guns.

In the early 1950's, Bob and Edith Sullivan purchased the property from the Wilson's, leasing the restaurant to Walter Ragsdales, who operated it for several years. As Eagle Nest Lake's popularity began to grow with the tourists, the Sullivan's advertised for college girls to help staff the lodge, restaurant, and saloon, as the small village of Eagle Nest could not provide the staffing needed for the popular tourist destination*. In 1964, the "new" hotel was built next to the original hotel for additional guests.

In 1971, Bert Clemens bought the property from the Sullivans and continues to operate it to this day. Bob and Edith Sullivan's son, Robert, stayed on in Eagle Nest for many years and was honored for his 25+ years as fire chief, councilor and mayor. Edith Sullivan, who operated the Laguna Vista for some twenty years, was honored as the Grand Marshall of the July 4th parade in 2003. Unfortunately, Mrs. Sullivan passed away on May 19, 2004.

So, does this old hotel and saloon have ghostly visitors similar to those at the St James Hotel in Cimarron, New Mexico, just a few miles down the road? Mr. Clemens says "yes," though he has never personally encountered them. At one point, a psychic visited the property who counted at least 22 spirits lingering around the place. One employee reported to Mr. Clemens, that while she was in the kitchen she heard the vacuum running in the dining room, but when she went to investigate no one was there and the vacuum was sitting still and silent.

The current manager, Jim, also indicates that eerie things happen, such as the piano in the dining room sometimes plays when no one is there, and a dining table chair is pulled up next to the piano. The staff will replace the chair next to one of the dining tables only to find it later back in front of the piano again.

Customers and staff have reported that a woman in dance-hall dress often appears, and then vanishes toward the site of the hidden staircase. This spirit is said be that of a woman on her honeymoon with her husband, enjoying a stay at the hotel. Her husband ventured out one day to go hunting and never returned. The distraught young woman was left stuck and destitute and was said to have become a saloon girl in order to provide for herself. Supposedly, it is her spirit that lingers at the hotel in search of her long lost husband.

An old staircase, which led from the Hotel Lobby to the upstairs rooms, has been boarded up. Most often the Ghost of Guney disappears at the site where this staircase used to be.

In talking with a former employee of the Laguna Vista, Kristi Dukes, who was a cook in the restaurant in 1999, she stated that she encountered several spooky visits from a spirit that is said to have once been a saloon girl in the old lodge. According to Kristi, both her and her mother Jane, who also worked in the restaurant, would often encounter these visits whenever the music they were listening to in the kitchen was anything other than classic rock or country music.

When Kristi, who often liked to listen to Rap, would change the music, strange things would occur. On one such occasion a marble rolling pin was thrown at Kristi, on other occasions pots and pans would fall off of the walls. Once, when odd things were happening, Jane asked Kristi to turn off the music but when she switched the stereo to the "off" position, the music continued to play. She then unplugged the stereo and, though it had no batteries, the music played on. Frightened, the two left at the end of the evening only to return the following day to a silent stereo.

The Laguna Vista Restaurant Dining Room.

It is in this room, which was once the hotel lobby that held the hidden staircase to the upstairs rooms, that the ghost is most often encountered. The spookiest story actually occurred when Kristi brought her daughter Rayni, who was 2 years old at the time, to work one day. She had placed little jingle bells on her daughter's shoes so that she could keep track of her while she was working. Suddenly, Rayni walked into the kitchen very gently and slowly. Kristi said she looked very odd and when she asked Rayni what was wrong, Rayni replied, "the lady told me to stop making noise". When Kristi asked Rayni where the lady was, Rayni led her mother into the dining room and pointed at "someone" saying "that lady." Kristi saw no one but Rayni insisted that her mother remove the bells from her shoes.

The locals say that the hotel caught fire about twenty years ago and closed, and that's about all they say. There's no doubt that the old hotel caught fire, because there are obvious signs of fire damage in two different locations at the old hotel. But, the question remains -- when?

And, was the fire the cause of the closing? At least one person has said that a later fire was started in a second location, probably by vagrants living in the old lodge. But, still neither fire has succeeded in demolishing this once wonderful luxury resort.

Just outside the front door, the lake beckoned the guests for fishing and boating, and to the right, are the remains of a man-made pool and a garden, as well as what appears to be stables. Several outbuildings are housed on the property, including private cabins and a caretaker's home.

So, what happened to this place? No one seems to know though it is said that when questioned on resident said that both his mother and aunt worked there, but they would not talk about what happened. However, at least one person from Angel Fire speculated that the place had become somewhat of a speakeasy with all manner of vices including gambling and prostitution and that was the reason the locals were reluctant to talk about it. However, this is just rumor and speculation with no basis in fact from anyone associated with the old lodge.

New Mexico State TB Sanitarium

Escondida, New Mexico

The New Mexico State TB Sanitarium was built by the Civilian Conservation Corps and opened its doors in 1932. It originally had 50 beds but was expanded to eventually have 1,200 beds. Several structures comprise the location. Originally the site looked like the spokes of a half of a wagon wheel, when viewed from the air.

The most predominant today are the dorms, where patients were housed. All together there were 9 wards for patients. The main hospital is now hidden back behind the NM State police headquarters. This building had an explosion proof operating room with glass block windows. There was also a kitchen, dining facility and a recreation hall where 16mm films were shown to staff and patients.

In the early years the hospital did well. Service was described as outstanding by patients and staff alike. However, that would eventually change.

By October 1952 many unfavorable reports about the hospital had been reported. Alva Simpson, in a letter to the state governor, claimed that the biggest problem was that patients released from the sanitarium had to be treated for improper nutrition and lack of sanitation. The facility was closed shortly afterwards.

The old hospital was converted and became a battery manufacturing plant named Eagle Pitcher. This factory operated for many years before being closed down.

Today, this historic old facility is abandoned, with piles of trash in most of the buildings. There is a bottle dump just west of the main site where there are mounds of old medicine bottles. The New Mexico State Police have also used the area as a shooting range, so spent brass from rounds fired by officers can be found around the dump area as well.

The area has changed greatly over the years. The major change is a road that now runs through the site. The New Mexico State Police have also built a regional headquarters near the old hospital.

THE GHOSTS

People have reported seeing glowing balls of light moving about the ruins of the sanitarium after dark. Unusual noises, to include, screams and shouts have also been heard coming from the old dorm buildings.

ST. James Hotel

Cimarron, New Mexico

The St. James Hotel began life as a small saloon in 1873. The two story hotel has been in continual operation since it was added to the saloon in 1880. Entering the St. James Hotel in Cimarron, New Mexico is like stepping back in time. The hallways of the guest area are decorated with deep red carpets, and red brocade wallpaper. The small ventilation windows above the doors are hand painted in different western scenes. Antiques, most original to the hotel, abound. Such wonderful pieces as 5 ft tall iron candelabra lamps, vintage chairs, a pump organ, even a roulette table that used to be in the gambling area of the original saloon, are scattered throughout the hallways. On the walls are framed photos of the famous guests the hotel once catered to.

The rooms are all named after former guests. For instance, repeat customers such as Buffalo Bill Cody, Jesse James, and Zane Gray, often chose to stay in the same room each time they visited. These rooms they were partial to now bear their names.

Figure 12: The St. James Hotel.

The history of this old hotel is equally as fascinating. In 1862, upon the recommendation of Ulysses S Grant, President Lincoln appointed a young Frenchman named Henry (formerly Henri) Lambert as his personal chef, a position Lambert held until that fateful day in 1865.

After Lincoln's assassination, Henry made his way west in search of gold. However, instead of discovering gold, he discovered he could make a very good living cooking for the miners in a small New Mexico boom town called Elizabethtown (E-Town). While passing through E-town, Lucien Maxwell, land baron of New Mexico Territory, had the opportunity to taste Henry Lambert's cooking. Lucien was so impressed he offered Lambert a job cooking for him in nearby Cimarron (Spanish for "wild" or "unbroken").

Henry accepted the offer and moved to Cimarron. In 1872, while still working for Lucien Maxwell, Henry began building Lambert's Saloon and Billiard Hall. It wasn't long before Lambert's Saloon became wildly popular, catering to the cowboys, traders, miners, frontiersman, and many others traveling this last leg of the Santa Fe Trail.

The Saloon did so well, in fact, that in 1880 Henri added 30 guest rooms and the St. James Hotel was born. The hotel, considered at the time to be one of the most elegant, luxurious hotels west of the Mississippi, soon became as popular as the saloon itself.

Before long the hotel guest registry read like a who's who of the Old West;

- Jesse James stayed there often, always in room 14 and always signing the registry with his alias, RH Howard
- Buffalo Bill Cody met Annie Oakley in Cimarron and they both stayed in the hotel while planning and rehearsing their Wild West Show. They took an entire village of Indians from the Cimarron area with them when they took the show on the road
- Wyatt Earp, his brother Morgan, and their wives spent 3 nights at the St. James on their way to

Tombstone. After leaving the hotel they made their way to the small town of Las Vegas, NM (about 30 miles southeast of Cimarron) where they met, and became friends with, a gentleman named J.J. "Doc" Holliday

- Zane Grey penned his novel "Fighting Caravans" while staying at the hotel
- Lew Wallace, Governor of New Mexico Territory, wrote part of Ben Hur there.

Other famous, and infamous, guests included Doc Holliday, Billy the Kid, Bat Masterson, Kit Carson, Clay Allison, and Pat Garret. Probably the most famous unknown person to stay at the hotel was Bob Ford. Doesn't ring a bell? Bob Ford's claim to fame was that he killed Jesse James.

Not surprisingly, with this combination of guests, the hotel boasts a violent history. At least 26 men were killed in gunfights at the hotel. The ceiling of the Saloon (currently the dining room) still has 22 original bullet holes in it. Luckily, when Henry built the hotel he had the foresight to add 3 feet of hard wood above the tin ceiling of the saloon to keep stray bullets from penetrating the floor of the upstairs guest rooms!

As times changed, railroads began taking the place of horse and buggy, mining and ranching became less profitable, and Cimarron's popularity begin to dwindle. Eventually, the once popular and elegant St. James Hotel fell into disrepair. Through the years it went largely uninhabited and passed from owner to owner until the mid 1980's when the beautiful old hotel was purchased and restored to its former luxury.

Today, the hotel is once again a hotel, but, much to its credit, it is far from being modern. There are no phones, no radios, and no televisions. Almost all of the furniture is original to the hotel, from the antique chandeliers, to the beds and dressers in the guest rooms. A stay at today's St. James Hotel is eerily similar to a stay during the heyday of the Wild West

THE GHOSTS

. The second floor of the hotel is the most active, with stories of cold spots and the smell of cigar smoke lingering in the halls. (Smoking is not allowed in the hotel.) A prior manager said that "you never see them, but you do feel and hear them." Another report from a former owner, states that she walked into the dining room and saw a pleasant-looking cowboy standing behind her in the mirror at the bar. The spiritual activity of the hotel has been featured on the popular television shows Unsolved Mysteries and A Current Affair.

Room 18

As the story goes, one night in 1881, the owner of the St. James was playing cards with some men in the 2nd floor card room. It was getting late, the men had imbibed a fair amount of whiskey, and the stakes were high. So high that, confidant he would win, the owner bet the hotel. However, a guest of the hotel, Mr. Thomas James (TJ) Wright also felt he had a winning hand and stayed in the game when all the others folded. When all bets were made and the cards were shown, TJ proved victorious. Satisfied with his win, TJ decided to retire for the night. As he made his way down the hall and began to turn the corner towards his room he was shot from behind. TJ continued on to his room, room 18, shut the door and slowly bled to death.

Perhaps the death of Thomas James Wright's was so traumatic that his spirit still remains locked in time. Whatever may be the reason, Room 18 is considered the most haunted room in the hotel. The room is considered so haunted, in fact, that nobody is allowed to enter the room, much less sleep in it. It is said that residing in the room is TJ's very angry, malevolent presence. The employees of the hotel say that no one is allowed in the room because whenever anyone goes in something bad happens in the hotel.

One former owner said she was pushed down while in the room and, on another occasion, saw a ball of angry orange light floating in the upper corner. The room holds only a bed frame without a mattress, a coat rack, a rocking chair and bureau which has been made a shrine to the Old West. Sitting atop the bureau is a Jack Daniels bottle, a basin and pitcher, a hand of cards, an Ace Copenhagen tin, and several shot glasses. On the wall is a bad painting of a half-naked woman.

Others have said that the real reason that the management will not let anyone sleep in Room 18 is that there has been more than the average number of mysterious deaths in the room.

For those of a doubting frame of mind, there was a Thomas James Wright born in New Mexico in 1859 and one of the old guest registries does show that a TJ Wright stayed in the hotel several nights in 1881.

The Mary Lambert Room

Another spirit is believed to be that of Mary Lambert, wife of Henry Lambert, the man who built the St.

James Hotel. She lived many years in the hotel, gave birth to her children there, watched at least 2 of her babies die there, and eventually, in December of 1926, died there herself. The people that work at the hotel call her the protector. They firmly believe her presence is still there and they believe she watches out for the hotel and the people in it.

It is said that you can often smell Mary's perfume when her presence is near, and many staff members, previous owners, and guests swear they have indeed smelled it. It is also said that if you are staying in her room and you leave the window open she will tap on it incessantly until you close it. On other occasions, a milky transparent woman can be seen in the hallways.

The Kate Lambert Room

The employees of The St. James are given the option of living in the hotel. One of the employees, a young lady, decided to stay in the hotel and was given the Kate Lambert Room which is the last room on the right at the end of the 2nd floor family wing. The room is directly across from the Mary Lambert room, and directly next to room 18.

The young lady has said the almost as son as she began to stay in the room, she had problem sleeping. Many times every night she would awaken, although there was nothing specific, such as a noise, that would explain her being awakened. Due to her lack of sleep, she was usually exhausted the next day.

Because of the hotel's history, ghost hunters and psychics often visit the hotel, so she asked one of the psychics to come to her room. The psychic told her that the spirit of TJ was trying to posses her. However, on the plus side, the spirit of Mary Lambert was protecting her from TJ.

The psychic told the tired young lady that it was this nightly spectral battle was what kept waking her up. The young employee liked the room in which she was staying very much and certainly did not want to move. However, the psychic told her that if she stayed in the room, eventually the spirit of TJ would eventually succeed and posses her. Just to be on the safe side, the young lady moved to another room and found that she slept soundly each night, no longer waking up in the early hours of the morning.

Non-Specific Hauntings

In addition to the well known spirits haunting the St. James, employees have reported that many non-specific hauntings occur on a daily basis. There are cold spots, things are constantly falling off of walls and shelves and the computer and phone at the front desk behave erratically. Cameras and video equipment often break or don't work correctly

The dining room, which used to be the main saloon, still houses the original mirrored bar. Many guests have reported seeing the reflection of a cowboy sitting at one of the tables only to look around and discover there is no one else in the room.

Hanging above the 2nd floor landing is a large crystal chandelier. During restoration, one of the previous owners discovered that every time she would turn it off before leaving, it would be on again by the time she got to the parking area. This happened repeatedly, even though there was no one in the hotel. Since they were in the process of restoration she thought maybe it was an electrical problem, but the electricians found nothing that could account for the light coming on by itself. Now the staff just leaves the ornate chandelier burning 24hrs a day.

One employee who was working the front desk reported that he very clearly heard a high pitched shriek coming from the far corner of the lobby. Looking up from his work, he was dumbfounded to see absolutely no one on that side of the room. Quickly looking around, his eyes rested on three other quests mingling at the other side of the lobby, apparently having not heard the loud scream, they were completely unphased.

The Annex

Apparently, the original hotel is not the only place with strange happenings. In the 1980's a modern 10 room annex was built onto the hotel. The rooms in the annex have all the amenities, including phones and cable TV.

It is said that there has been unexplained activity in the annex. According to one employee there were two girls staying in one of the room in the annex who had an unusual experience.

It seems that one of the girls was taking a shower when the other girl opened the bathroom door. The girl in the shower yelled for her friend to close the door and let her finish her shower. The door shut, but a few minutes later it opened again. By the time the girl got out of the shower this had happened 3 or 4 times. Angry, the wet girl wrapped a towel around her and stormed out of the bathroom prepared to yell at her friend for continuing to open and shut the door. To her surprise, her friend was not in the room. She finally talked to her friend, the girl that had been in the shower discovered that whoever or whatever had been opening and closing the shower door, it was not her friend as she had not even been in the room at the time.

There is also another, though, friendly, spirit known to inhabit this old hotel. The owners have dubbed this spirit the "little imp", as it likes to torment new employees in the kitchen and dining room. Described as a small man with a pockmarked face, the little imp has been known to burst glasses, re-light candles, and move objects in front of nervous new hires.

The Plaza Hotel

Las Vegas, NM

Byron T. Mills was 3 prominent Las Vegas attorney and abstracter who owned the Plaza Hotel during most of the first half of this century. He arrived in Las Vegas in 1852, just after the landmark hotel was completed, and took over ownership of the property some 36 years later. According to the January, 1945 issue of New Mexico Magazine, Mills was beginning to dismantle the hotel and sell its furniture in anticipation of demolishing the three-story structure. The article neglected to explain his motives, but devoted considerable space to Mills' knowledgeable discourse on the hotel's history. Mills was even quoted as saying, "I almost feel guilty [about the demolition]. It certainly is an old landmark."

For reasons unknown today, Mills never followed through with his plan. Some speculate a disembodied "Byron T." haunts the hotel today out of a sense of guilt while others believe he remains because he loved the hotel more than he claimed in life. A third faction suggests the historic hotel's resident ghost simply enjoys the company of others, especially women, which may explain both the reported presence of a man coupled with the sudden scent of perfume.

THE GHOSTS

A number of the stories of hauntings seem to come from room 310. More than one lady traveling alone has reported the presence of a man in their room. Almost everyone would agree that the spirit of Mills has a special fondness for women who are alone in their rooms and traveling salesmen.

One particular salesman had checked into his room on the third floor, dropped his bags, and went directly to the bathroom. When he got out he noticed the door's dead bolt was locked. That's funny, he thought I don't remember locking the door. He then undressed for his shower, carefully putting his money under his clothes, neatly piled next to the sink. When he got out of the shower, he was startled to find his money now on top of his clothes!

Another employee who was staying in one of the third floor rooms for a time tells that she was awakened in the early morning hours by a door opening and footsteps across the room. Then she felt someone sit on the bed. She sat up, and saw nothing. She tried to go back to sleep, but until 5:00 am, when her husband finally returned, she heard Byron pacing back and forth across the room.

Other employees report smelling cigar smoke in the bar, and hearing heavy boots walking when there was no one there.

The hotel bar was also the scene of another of Byron's pranks. According to one story, there were a couple of devout Catholics, who after church one Good Friday, decided to go to the bar for drinks. They were sitting on the patio, feeling a little guilty to be spending that holy day in such a frivolous way, when a drop of blood fell out of nowhere, landing on a white tablecloth. They fled in horror, and have not indulged in liquor on Good Friday again.

The Lodge

Cloudcroft, New Mexico

The Lodge was originally constructed in the rustic mountain community of Cloudcroft, New Mexico in 1899, by the Alamogordo & Sacramento Mountain Railway. It was owned and operated by the railroad and intended to be a resort for workers who were the by-product of the railway's search for timber.

The hotel was immediately successful- it's breathtaking location in the lushly wooded Sacramento Mountains offered a welcome cool retreat to literally thousands of heat-punished Texans (New Mexico, Oklahoma, and Arizona were not yet states at this time). An article published in the Albuquerque Journal-Democrat near the completion of the Lodge in 1899 stated, "This beautiful building will be known as Cloudcroft Lodge and its interior will be furnished with a lavish hand, yet in keeping with the character of the place. Fireplaces, with wide, hungry mouths, will sparkle, crackle and dart forth welcome tongues of flame to hundreds of merry guests, who will find new pleasure in life during the long, sultry summer."

In 1908 the El Paso & Southwestern Railroad System- the Lodge's new owner- advertised that the hotel, restaurant, dancing pavilion, tennis court, golf links, bowling alley, billiard parlor, burro trips and children's playground were accessible for "weekend rates of $3.00 round trip," and that Lodge rates were "$12.50 and up" per week.

On June 13th 1909, a raging fire blazed through the Lodge, utterly destroying it. By 1911, the Lodge was completely rebuilt and reopened on its current site, and its appearance has remained virtually the same since then- a historic, timeless gem suspended in time. Over the long, distinguished history of the Lodge, it has played host to numerous famous folk- including Pancho Villa, Gilbert Roland, Judy Garland and Clark Gable (in fact the last two carved their names into the wall of the Lodge's Tower, where they can still be seen to this day). But by far the most infamous guest of all at the Lodge is the specter of Rebecca.

THE GHOSTS

Rebecca has become one of the most famous ghosts in New Mexico. The lovely young lady was a chambermaid at the Lodge who reputedly disappeared from the premises sometime in the 1920's/30's. They claim that this restless wraith has made her presence known here ever since her

Figure 13: This is believed to be a photo of Rebecca.

death.

Rebecca was said to be a gorgeous red-haired chambermaid who worked and lived at the Lodge in the 1920's/30's. Similar to her fellow Lodge employees, she lived in the employee's rooms, which were located in the basement at the time. She was by all means a very friendly and flirtatious young lady, and unforgettably lovely.

There was some rumor that Rebecca moonlighted as a prostitute, although no proof of this claim existed. Whatever the case, according to the story, Rebecca's jealous lumberjack boyfriend caught her in the arms of another man at the Lodge (possibly in Room 101, aka the Governor's Suite) and became enraged. Shortly after, Rebecca disappeared from the Lodge, never to be seen again. Well, not alive, anyway. Because soon after her disappearance people began to report having some very strange, even ghostly, experiences...

Over the years, there have been many sightings of an auburn haired apparition floating through the halls, a vision seen by both employees and guests alike. One guest heard scraping sounds in the hallway late one night and opened the door to see a red-haired woman in a 30's style night dress rearranging flowers in a vase on top of an antique chest.

Another guest was shocked when he went to take a shower, only to find a "vaporous female" reclining in his bathtub. There have also been reports of objects such as watches, ashtrays, and silverware sliding across surfaces untouched... doors opening and closing on their own...

lights and other appliances turning on and off by themselves... furniture moved inexplicably... and even faucets turning on and toilets flushing for no apparent reason.

But perhaps one of the strangest events happened one Halloween night, when a man dressed in a tuxedo came into the Lodge's dining room and sat alone at an intimate, two-chaired table. He ordered two dinners and two glasses of wine. Everyone in the room watched closely as the man ate his meal and carried on a conversation with someone who wasn't there. No one ever saw anyone sit with the man or even go near him, yet at the end of his meal, both wineglasses and both plates were empty.

Rebecca's manifestations are many. One of her favorite "hangouts" is the Red Dog Saloon- an old-west style saloon with rough-hewn walls and Southwest decorum- which is located in the basement, where the employee's showers used to be. This is a very active spot as the lights go off and on untouched. Even more mysteriously, 1930's-era poker chips have been mysteriously found in the middle of a floor which had been clear only minutes before. Ashtrays move by themselves and flames appear in the fireplace with no logs or other source of fuel.

Lodge patrons have called the front desk to complain about the loud music coming from the saloon at times when the saloon was empty and wasn't even open. Others have reported seeing an apparition of a twirling woman has been reportedly seen on the dance floor. One bartender claimed to have seen the reflection of a beautiful red-haired woman wearing a long dress in the mirror behind the bar- yet the woman wasn't there when the bartender turned around to look at her.

Another paranormal hotspot seems to be found in the "Tower"... a three-story structure that stands tall above the Lodge itself. The Tower is kept locked, with two levels of small sitting rooms with windows that yield a panoramic view of the lush mountains. Some have reported feeling cold spots and a "presence" in the Tower, and the third floor- which is where the locked door leading to the Tower can be found- is reportedly very paranormally active as well.

Additionally, there is also said to be a lot of activity surrounding Room 101, the Governor's Suite. Some have theorized that Rebecca carried on her "trysts" in this room and was perhaps even caught in the act there by her lumberjack boyfriend one fateful day. Whatever the connection, the Lodge staff has gotten calls from Room 101 where no one is on the other end, even when no one is in the room at the time. Despite having a modern, computerized phone system, the phone calls from Room 101 persist.

The light in the ceiling fan just outside of Room 101 is also said to turn off and on at will. A former housekeeper claimed that after making up a bed, she would come back only to find an indentation as if someone had just laid or sat there. She also said that guest's shoes would mysteriously move a few rooms down from where they were supposed to be. It would seem that even in spectral form Rebecca is a very fun-loving and mischievous spirit.

To this day, employees and guests alike are still reporting strange and mysterious encounters at the Lodge. There have been a number of reports that the toilets in the ladies room had been flushing by themselves earlier that very day. Whether you believe in Rebecca or not, the Lodge is still an amazing, unique place with a ton of fascinating history. The forest scenery and mountain views are heavenly, and the Lodge itself is a graceful and timeless treat lavishly furnished with the Victorian and country lodge decor of a bygone era. There is even a fabulous restaurant called- what else?- Rebecca's

Val Verde Hotel

Socorro, New Mexico

Built in 1915, the Val Verde is not as large as other hostelries in New Mexico, but from a stand point of beauty and convenience, she stands without a peer. It contains sixty guest rooms, a commodious dining room, a kitchen, a spacious lobby and writing rooms. With the exception of a few "grander" suites, the rooms share two common bathrooms located on the second floor. Each room is equipped with its own shower.

In present times the rooms are rented out as apartments, with two of the old rooms composing one apartment. The kitchen and dining room were converted to a restaurant while the old lobby is now a bar. Inside the building, one stair case leads to the upper floor. This door is locked so access to the second floor is by two fire escapes located at the rear of the building. These are also the stairs that the tenants use for access to their apartments.

THE GHOSTS

Figure 14: The front of the Valverde Hotel.

A great deal of activity takes place in the stairs leading to the second floor. Randomly flashing lights and small orbs (called globules) can be seen whisking about with Infrared cameras. The activity only seems to take place when a live band is playing, and even then only if it is "earth based" music with such instruments as violins and harmonicas. Perhaps sound vibrations somehow summons the spirits from where they normally reside.

Others have said that the spirit of an unidentified woman has also been seen on the stairs and landing. Though efforts have been made to identify this unknown figure, to date no one has been able to give her a name.

During its long history, a total of 10 people have died in various locations within the hotel. Five of these deaths were thought to be suicides.

Fort Craig was one of a number of military posts built prior to the Civil War to protect the settlers from marauding Indians. It also came to prominence during the

Figure 15: One of the Ruined Walls at Fort Craig.

abortive Confederate invasion of New Mexico. When the eleven states seceded from the Union in 1861 and formed the Confederate States of America. The Confederacy was desperately short of raw materials for war production. Those materials had to be imported from abroad and often paid for in gold. Gold and seaports became very important to the South.

The Confederacy was very much aware that California and the Western part of North America held both seaports and gold, and the South wanted them. A plan was devised to allow the Confederacy to both achieve the means to purchase raw materials and also to cut the government of the United States off from its western territories. In the summer of 1861, the 2nd Texas Regiment, Mounted Rifles, led by Lt. Col. John Baylor seized control of the Mesilla Valley (near present day Las Cruces) and declared New Mexico a Confederate territory. In the winter of 1861 a Confederate brigade invaded New Mexico with the hope of fulfilling the South's ambitions in the west.

The brigade was commanded by General Henry H. Sibley, formerly of the United States Army. It was comprised of three regiments of cavalry - the 4th, 5th, and 7th Texas Mounted Volunteers - and independent battery of artillery, totaling almost 3000 men and at least 18 cannons.

Opposing the Sibley Brigade were a few companies of the 5th and 7th US Infantry, a few companies of the 2nd Cavalry, a battalion of the 3rd Cavalry, a few batteries of artillery, one company of Colorado Volunteers, several regiments of New Mexico Volunteers, and some untrained militia. The overall commander of the U.S. forces was Col. Edward Canby.

The first battle of the campaign was south of Socorro, near Ft. Craig, at Val Verde ford. The Texans drove the Federal forces from the field and captured a battery of cannons in the savage encounter that saw the only documented use of lancers in the War Between the States.

Canby retreated into Ft. Craig though, and Sibley could not get him out. The Texans lost many supply wagons to a surprise cavalry charge by the New Mexico Volunteers. Short on supplies, Sibley chose to bypass Ft. Craig and continue north toward Albuquerque.

Albuquerque was occupied on March 2, 1862 and Santa Fe five days later. The Confederates were critically short of food and other supplies, and needed the Federal stores at Ft. Union on the Santa Fe Trail north of Las Vegas. At Ft. Union there were about 1300 Federal troops, including several companies of Regulars and New Mexico Volunteers, but mainly the newly organized 1st Colorado Volunteers, known as "Pike's Peakers". The 1st Colorado had arrived at Ft. Union after a Herculean effort, including a march through a blizzard. The fort and its troops were commanded by Col. John Slough. Slough's orders from Canby were to protect Ft. Union at all costs, but not to start a major battle. Slough thought the best place from which to defend Ft. Union was on the road to Santa Fe, so he started down the road toward Glorietta Pass.

On the 26th of March, a force of about 400 Confederates under the command of Maj. Charles Pyron was scouting the western end of Glorietta Pass, called Apache Canyon. They came around a bend and ran into Slough's advanced party of about 415 men under the command of Maj. Chivington. Chivington attacked at once and drove the Confederates down the canyon in a wild running fight and captured dozens of Texans. Fearing the entire Confederate brigade was nearby he halted his men and withdrew to Kozlowski's Ranch near Pecos. Maj. Pyron fell back to "wood and water", two critical items in New Mexico during the early spring and sent for help. His courier found Lt. Col. William Scurry at Galisteo, just going into camp with two battalions of the brigade. Within minutes Scurry put his men on the road to Apache Canyon. An all night march through bitter cold brought them to Pyron's position about dawn. The Texans prepared for a Federal Assault and waited throughout the 27th.

At Kozlowski's, Slough and Chivington decided on their plan of attack. Slough would take about 2/3rd of the troops' including all the artillery, down the pass toward Santa Fe. Chivington would take his battalion of 113, guided by Lt. Col. J. Francisco Chaves of the New Mexico Volunteers over the shoulder of Glorietta Mesa and fall upon the Confederate flank. The plan was set in motion on the morning of the 28th.

Scurry had decided not to wait at Apache Canyon. He started almost all of his force, including Pyron's men, eastward through the pass. He left his supply wagons with a small guard at Johnson's Ranch at the junction of Glorietta pass and Apache Canyon. Around mid morning he hit Slough's lead elements near Pigeon's Ranch, located on the Santa Fe Trail. Scurry deployed his men in a long line and set his artillery up on a low hill. Slough did the same though his line was shorter than Scurry's since Scurry's force had over 300 men more than Slough.

Scurry's battalions attacked with great vigor but were met with equal vigor by the Coloradoans. Slough's position was not strong, but the attack was stopped long enough to give his men time to fall back to a better one. Slough tried to send men to his right around Scurry's flank but a detachment of Texans met his men head on and stopped them. Scurry kept pressure on Slough's line while organizing his own force in a three pronged assault. Late in the afternoon the Confederates attacked Slough's entire front driving in the flanks and threatening the center. The outnumbered Federal infantry held the Texans at bay long enough for the artillery to pull back to a third line. Scurry's men pursued, but were exhausted from the six hour battle.

Slough soon abandoned this line leaving the Confederates in undisputed possession of the field.

While all this was going on at Pigeon's Ranch Chivington had completely missed Scurry's flank falling instead on the Confederate supply train parked at Apache Canyon. Lightly guarded the train was captured and destroyed leaving Scurry with no ammunition, food blankets, or other supplies. Chivington returned to Kozlowski's and Slough's reunited command continued in withdrawal toward Ft. Union. Unable to sustain his men in the field Scurry was forced to go back to Santa Fe where Sibley joined him.

Canby had left Ft. Craig early in April and had come north threatening Albuquerque and drawing Sibley's entire force back from Santa Fe. Canby and Slough united their forces east of the Sandia Mountains and now outnumbered the Texans. Sibley faced with superior numbers and even more destitute than before knew that to stay and fight would mean destruction of his brigade. He decided to retreat from New Mexico. The Confederacy never again seriously threatened the far west.

The hardships endured by men on both sides in New Mexico were unbelievable. Sibley's campaign covered 2000 miles and his men originally equipped as cavalry walked more than half the route. The Colorado Volunteers on their march from Colorado City to Ft. Union set the standard for endurance by troops anywhere. Starvation, thirst, cold heat and disease killed more men on both sides than did bullets. The battles fought in and around Val Verde and Glorietta though tiny by eastern standards were as viciously and brutally contested as Gettysburg. The men who faced the bullets were as brave, hurt as badly and were as mourned as deeply as their comrades elsewhere.

THE GHOSTS

I have been to a number of old military posts in the research for my books. In each I have felt a sense of purpose as if something about those who once served this country still remained. So do does it seem that those who garrisoned Fort Craig and tried to stop the depredations of both marauding Indians as well as the Confederate forces still stand ready to defend their country and the walls of Fort Craig.

Some who have visited Fort Craig late in the evening report, as they approach, seeing figures that appear to be blue clad sentries. However, when they arrive at the site, there is no one to be seen. One individual reported that he was there about dusk and he was absolutely sure that he had heard the faint sounds of taps floating on the breeze.

Figures and glowing orbs have been sighted around the Commander's Quarters and along Officers Row. I am told that one group set up a tape recorder and recorded the sounds of a voice counting cadence as the rhythmic sounds of men marching could be heard in the background. There was also the sound of bits jingling and leather creaking.

Just as I found at Fort Bliss, Texas, apparently there are those who will not leave their posts until the great commander properly relieves them of their duty.

There have been a number of reports that gun shorts have been heard and several have been very adamant that the gunshots came from muskets. Others have reported what sounds like canon fire.

I have also read reports that some witnesses have smelled the distinctive aroma of black powder. When someone fires a black powder pistol or rifle, there is a distinctive smell that is unmistakable.

NEVADA

Austin

Sometimes unusual incidents are the reason good things happen. Such is the case with the little town of Austin, NV. The silver deposits that gave birth to the town

Figure 16: International Hotel

were actually discovered in 1862 by a horse belonging to a W. H. Talbot. The horse, by accident, kicked up a piece of quartz containing gold and silver. Talbot sent the piece to Virginia City for assay. He staked out a claim and, when word got out, others followed, and a silver rush was on. By 1880, the mines began to show signs of exhaustion and its total of $50 million in ore production was history. Once so difficult to reach, Austin is now immediately accessible on highway 50. It was one of the early Nevada mining towns and has remained comparatively unspoiled.

In addition to the history that can be glimpsed along the streets of this remnant of the past, there are also ghosts that are said to haunt some of the old buildings. One of these buildings is the old International Hotel.

International Hotel

The history of the International Hotel is certainly interesting. The author has been told that the building that became the hotel was originally erected in Virginia City, Nevada before being moved to Austin in 1862. In fact this building is said to be the oldest in Nevada. Many concerts and large balls were held upstairs in the Grand Ball Room. Emma Nevada, world famous European opera singer, made her debut appearance here to a sold out audience. Today this historic old landmark is known as the International Café & Bar and is said to serve outstanding food.

In addition to the food and spirits it serves by day there is said to be a number of spirits that haunt the old hotel by night. The primary ghost is called Tommy and is believed to be the spirit of a former owner or perhaps an employee. Tommy is said to often be seen or his presence felt at the end of the bar and it can be heard stomping around upstairs in the old hotel.

Boulder City Hotel

There are a few individuals who seem able to see into the future. One of these was a man by the name of Jim Webb. When word began to circulate about the huge project being undertaken, he had a vision of what Boulder City needed: a grande dame hotel with unprecedented private baths, air conditioning, and a gumwood paneled lobby that would accommodate world dignitaries visiting the Boulder Dam.

Webb's vision became a reality and during the 1930s the Boulder Dam Hotel was a huge draw for people visiting Boulder Dam

Figure 17: Boulder City Hotel

and movie stars who needed to establish Nevada residency so they could obtain a "quickie" divorce. The building was truly one of the most elegant, modern hotels in the western United States, and the gala grand opening was unlike any extravaganza attended by the elite society.

Some of the famous guests during 1934 included A.P. Gianni, founder of Bank of America, Bette Davis, who stayed at the hotel while on vacation following the filming of, "Of Human Bondage," and the cast and crew of RKO films, who stayed while they produced the movie, "Silver Streak." During 1935, a few more of the famous guests staying at the hotel included honeymooners Mr. and Mrs. Cornelius Vanderbilt, Jr., Will Rogers, who was performing on stage at the Boulder Theatre, the Maharajah and Maharani of Indore, India, and Cardinal Pascelli, who later became Pope Pius XII. Throughout the remainder of the 1930s, other famous guests who included a trip to the great damn on their travels included the Duchess of Westminster, George Pepperdine, founder of Pepperdine University, Henry Fonda, Boris Karloff, Senator Robert Taft, Shirley Temple, and Howard Hughes, who recuperated at the hotel after wrecking his airplane on Lake Mead.

What was interesting is that some of these guests have never checked out. There have been many reports of apparitions, some of them very recognizable people.

Bee Hive Whorehouse

Most places where there have been large amounts of activity seem to retain the imprint of those who spent a great deal of time there. Certain a brothel would qualify as a place where folks spent a great deal of time. In Carson City there was a brothel known as the Bee Hive Whorehouse that is known to be haunted by those who have gone before.

The ghost of a tall, bloated woman with straggly red hair and dressed in a dirty, white nightgown has been seen on the streets near the whorehouse where she once lived and plied her trade. Her name is Timber Kate, and she was part of a notorious saloon act with her female lover, Bella Rawhide. The two performed live sex acts in honky-tonks in Carson City, Spokane, Butte, and Cheyenne. But the young Bella fell in love with a half-breed ruffian by the name of Tug Daniels. After Bella and Tug ran away together, Timber Kate resorted to dressing as a man in white tights and lifting weights on stage, though she usually ended doing a bizarre strip-tease.

In 1880, Bella and Tug met up with Kate in Carson City. In the ensuing showdown, Tug pulled a knife and cut open Kate's belly "from her crotch to her navel." The eviscerated woman died in excruciating pain on the whorehouse floor. Tug escaped and was never seen again. In 1882, Bella committed suicide by drinking cleaning fluid. The site of the old Bee Hive Whorehouse is on north Quincy Street, but Timber Kate's ghost has been seen on many of the streets nearby.

Amargosa Opera House & Hotel

Figure 18: Amargosa Hotel and Opera House

What is now known as the Amargosa Opera House & Hotel began life as a community center known as Corkhill Hall. Corkhill Hall has been converted into a hotel which contained a theatre now named the Amargosa Hotel. In 1967 it was pretty much deserted when a dancer from New York, Marta Becket came upon it en route to an engagement. She was smitten by the possibilities of the ruined theatre, built the year she was born.

On a shoestring, she first leased, and then bought the complex. Benefactors helped— the Amargosa is now owned by a non-profit organization—but it was she who provided the energy to restore the theatre and hotel. Her personality permeates everything, and makes a visit there a special experience.

Along with a hotel and theatre, Marta also seems to have purchased several ghosts, at least according to a number of psychics and the local tales. Among the tales of ghosts and hauntings are:

- According to legends, in an unused area of the hotel which was actually a mine shaft where employees of the Pacific Coast Borax Company have lived, there had been either a murder or a suicide.
- In room 34, it was reported that a little girl named Mary was murdered. When you enter the room, it is possible to see a tall figure by the window what was said to be the killer. Guests who have merely walked past the door to room 34 also report a strange feeling.
- The theatre itself is also said to be haunted. Most people upon entering the theatre report feeling a very unusual sensation said to be linked to the ghost.

There are many stories about this historic old hotel and opera house. The owner seems content to allow them to continue to stay there, but many have come to visit. Even Criss Angel did a show segment from the old hotel that aired October 31, 2006.

Goldfield Hotel

The Goldfield Hotel is closed off and abandoned with no access to the public. You can walk around the front along sidewalks, look in windows, etc. It has been partially remodeled over the years in a failed casino conversion project. Perhaps someday an investor with enough funds will follow through and restore it properly but so much major work has already been done to alter it for other projects, it would be difficult to restore.

Built on top of an abandoned gold mine, this 154-room hotel was opened in 1908. The hotel is considered home to several ghosts. In the downstairs employees' area, Room 109 is a small room with a single bed. The room is haunted by the presence of a pregnant

Figure 19: Goldfield Hotel

woman. Psychics have seen her ghost chained to a radiator there. Rumors say a pregnant prostitute named Elizabeth was chained in the room by George Winfield, the original owner of the hotel. After giving birth, the woman was left to die in the room and the baby was thrown down the old mine shaft at the northern end of the basement. Elizabeth's ghost even turned up on a photograph taken in the room by a reporter from Las Vegas.

On the first floor, the George Winfield Room is said to be haunted by his ghost. Untraceable cigar smoke and fresh ashes have been found there. George's presence has also been detected near the Lobby Staircase, where the ghosts of a midget and two small children have also been seen. The Gold Room is haunted by a ghost that "stabs" people. High psychic energy is been detected in the Theodore Roosevelt Room and a southwest room on the third floor. Some psychics say that the Goldfield Hotel is one of only seven portals to the Other Side that exist in the modern world.

Gold Hill Hotel

Figure 20: Gold Hill Hotel

Built in 1859 as the Riesen House, the Gold Hill Hotel is the oldest operating hotel and saloon in the state of Nevada. It is located just outside of Virginia City. Visitors arriving to Virginia City from either the Lake Tahoe or Reno areas pass by this small town en route to Virginia

City. It is also a stop on the 35 minute train tour of the Virginia and Truckee Railroad tour.

H. M. Vesey acquired the hotel early in the 1860's and added the wooden structure to the original stone building. The hotel became an important part of the now thriving metropolis of Gold Hill which was adjacent to the even larger industrial and business center known as Virginia

At least two ghosts are said to reside here. First, there is William, a firefighter who died in the Yellow Jacket fire. Guests at the hotel have been known to smell his pipe tobacco. He particularly hangs out in room # 5 and has repeatedly awakened guests at 3:00 o'clock in the morning by shaking the bed.

There is also the ghost of Rosie. Rosie is believed to be a previous housekeeper who enjoys moving guests' keys around. A visitor can know when Rosie is present by the smell of old fashioned rose petals.

Aladdin Hotel and Casino

Figure 21: Aladdin Hotel & Casino

The hotel that was known as the Aladdin Hotel for much of its life was the first major casino to open on the Las Vegas strip in the 1960s, but throughout its history it has been known by a number of names and had a number of owners. There were many who claim that this hotel has always had a cloud hanging over it as well as its owners.

This hotel originally opened in 1963 as the Tally-Ho. In late 1964 it became known as the Kings Crown, but this business failed within six months when it was not able to get a gaming license. In 1966 the new and improved Aladdin Hotel and Casino was opened with a very upscale Arabian Nights theme.

There are a number of interesting stories told about the Aladdin Hotel and Casino. Many guests complained that during the night they would hear the sound of a key being inserted into the door lock and whispering coming from the hallway. Of course, like most hotels in Vegas, the room doors use electronic cards, not keys and the old fashion locks have not been used in years.

Many of these stories of hauntings seem to revolve around the Panorama Suite on the seventh floor. According to many, visitors staying in the Panorama Suite have also heard strange whispering and the sounds of a key being inserted into the door lock. The Panorama Suite also had, the Aladdin has now been demolished, a door buzzer which rings at the oddest hours. When the door is answered, of course, there is never anyone there. Items have also been known to vanish from the suite and reappear in other places.

MGM Grand Hotel and Casino/Bally's Hotel &Casino

Figure 22: MGM Lion

The original MGM Grand Hotel and Casino began life as the Marina Hotel. The Marina Hotel, located at 3805 Las Vegas Boulevard, opened in 1975 as a 714 room hotel and casino. In 1989 Kirk Kerkorian bought the Marina Hotel and the Tropicana Country Club to obtain the site that would become the home of the MGM Grande the largest hotel in the world. At the time of the fire, the MGM Grand had 2,100 rooms and about 91% of the rooms were occupied on that particular day. There were over 5,000 people in the hotel and the casino at the time of the fire. In addition to the hotel and the casino located on the property were five restaurants and a shopping mall. So the face that there were only 5,000 people on the property was a minor miracle in and of itself. Of course there were a number of unexpected occupants in the hotel, a number of thieves took advantage of the confusion and came into the hotel on a robbery run, an undetermined number of them died in the fire.

Compounding the problems with the smoke and flames was the fact that the hotel and casino had been designed by some of the best decorators in Hollywood. As a result, a lot of plastic had been used, plastic which released toxic fumes when ignited. As a result, guests and staff who were nowhere near the scene of the fire died as a result of the toxic gas filtering through the air system. A number of gamblers were so intent o MGM Grand. During that time, the Marina was known as the MGM-Marina Hotel.

Ground was broken on October 7, 1991 for the new casino hotel

Figure 23: The new Lion

complex. The Marina closed on November 30, 1991. The Marina hotel building still exists as the western end of the main hotel building. The modern Bally's Hotel and Casino is built on the location that used to be the MGM Hotel which gained international recognition as a result of a terrible fire which killed a number of staff and guests. On the corner of Flamingo and Las Vegas Boulevard, where Bally's now stands, the MGM once had a glamorous hotel and casino. On November 21, 1980, it burned to the ground. It was a horrific, tragic event, with some guest jumping to their death when rescue ladders could not reach their upper floor windows. Over 500 people were injured and a total of 84 people died that day, and two more over the next few months, making it the second largest hotel fire in terms of lives lost in United States history.

Eventually a new hotel-casino was erected at the site of this devastating tragedy. And though Bally's is owned and operated by a different company, but built in the footprint of the MGM none of the original MGM remains, the spirits of the people who died so tragically in 1980 are said to still linger at the location where they died. Try a tour of Bally's hotel corridors at night; you may run into some ghostly guests who have never quite checked out.

As might be guessed, it is believed that many of the ghosts of the ghosts that walk the halls of MGM/Bally's stem from that tragic fire that almost destroyed the hotel in November of 1980.

The heat and fire were so intense that the front doors of the hotel were blown completely off their hinges and the cars parked outside the entrance were completely destroyed. According to newspaper reports, there was a cloud of smoke the rose over a mile into the sky. The crystal chandeliers and ceiling panels in the casino all crashed to the floor as a wall of flame swept through the first floor.

Later investigation showed that the fire began with a spark caused by an electrical ground fault in the wiring that sent power to a compressor located under a pie display case in The Deli, one of the small restaurants at the MGM Grand. This initial fire caused smoke to spread rapidly through the buildings air conditioning system.

The ghosts of the MGM Grand slowly began to make themselves known over the next eight months as the new Bally's took shape. Though everything was new the old would not go away. It was said to be like the old hotel superimposed over the new and it led to some startling happenings.

According to a number of witnesses there have been quite a number of incidents involving guests and staff at the Bally's seeing entities from the disaster at the MGM Grande. The desk clerks have had a number of calls from guests about strange sights in their rooms.

Dunes Hotel and Casino/Bellagio

The Dunes opened on May 23, 1955, as a low-rise resort with Hollywood star Vera-Ellen providing the entertainment in the Magic Carpet Review. When the North Tower was added in 1961 it was one of the finest and largest hotels on the strip. The South Tower was added in 1979. The hotel was built in part with financing from movie mogul Al Gottesman and the Teamsters Pension Fund. The resort boasted an 18-hole golf course, a rooftop health spa and a 90 ft (27 m)-long pool. The Hotel's Slogan was "The Miracle in the Desert."

In its early years, the Dunes was known for the 35 ft tall fiberglass sultan (1964) that stood above its main entrance. Many top performers, such as Dean Martin, Liberace, George Burns, Pat Cooper, Judy Garland, Phyllis Diller, and Frank Sinatra have performed at the hotel.

Although it opened to much fanfare, it struggled from the start: one reason was its location at what was then the southernmost part of the Strip. The hotel frequently had

Figure 24: Dunes Hotel and Casino

to borrow money, and even the Sands Hotel lent its executives to help out, as well as bringing in numerous famous celebrities and entertainers such as Frank Sinatra's surprise appearance dressed as a sultan. On January 10, 1957, in a desperate move to keep the resort afloat, the Dunes became the first hotel/casino in Nevada to offer a topless show, called Minsky's Follies - the first of which was "Minsky Goes to Paris." The State Legislature was "in an uproar," but the show set a record for attendance in a single week at 16,000. In 1961, a 24 story tower was built, bringing the number of rooms up to 450. In 1970, there were unrealized rumors Howard Hughes would buy into the hotel. In 1979, the hotel expanded to 1300 rooms. The sultan statue, by now on the golf course, caught fire in 1985, reportedly due to an electrical short in its stomach. In 1987, Japanese investor Masao Nangaku purchased the Dunes "for $155 million but could not make it a financial success".

On November 17, 1992, the Dunes was sold for the last time to developer Steve Wynn's company, Mirage Resorts, Inc. for $75 million. On January 26, 1993, the Dunes closed its doors for good. Though once of the finest and most grand hotels on the strip, like many of the legendary properties of its era, it could no longer compete with the newer and more exciting megaresorts that were being built.

By the time the hotel was closed guests routinely reported feeling cold spots in a number of locations throughout the hotel especially in the main tower and the casino. There were also a number of stories about the lounge on the top floor of the Dunes. A number of guests and workers reported blue glows being seen in several areas and the sounds of voices coming from empty rooms.

There was also the story of the young Keno Runner who was in the wrong place at the wrong time. From all accounts she was a very pretty young with a bubbly personality. Everyone liked her and was sure that she was destined for bigger and better things. But sometimes things don't work out like we plan. She walked into a convenience store robbery and was killed. Friends and co-workers mourned, but soon it was business as usual. Then the sightings happened. She was seen in the casino restaurant, at the Keno desk, and often she was seen just moving about the hotel.

In 1993 the Dunes was imploded and in its place rose the Bellagio, one of the most eye catching hotel/casinos in Las Vegas. But in spite of its ultra modern façade, even the Bellagio has a ghost that is all its own. In July of 1994 actor Justin Pierce was staying at the hotel. The young actor was newly married, a new father and a rising star. He was in Las Vegas to do a photo shoot and by all reports was in good spirits. However, one morning he was found hanging in his room, an apparent suicide. Whatever may have been the cause or reason for his death, Justin Pierce has been seen walking the halls of the Bellagio, perhaps searching for the peace in death he did not find in life.

Caesar's Palace Hotel Casino

In 1962, Jay Sarno, a cabana motel owner, used US$35 million that had been lent to him by the Teamsters Central States Pension Fund to begin plans for a hotel on land owned by Kirk Kerkorian. Sarno would later act as designer of the hotel he planned to construct.

Figure 25: Caesar's Palace

Building of the 14-story Caesars Palace hotel began in 1962. That first tower would have 680 rooms on the 34 acre (138,000 m2) site.

Sarno struggled to decide on a name for the hotel. He finally decided to call it Caesars Palace because he thought that the name Caesar would evoke thoughts of royalty because of Roman general Julius Caesar. Also he felt the name would attract a more seductive crowd of women to attract more men into the gambling portion of the casino. Sarno felt that guests should feel they were at a king's home while at his hotel. It is called "Caesars" and not "Caesar's" because every guest is a Caesar.

Sarno contracted many companies to build the hotel, from the Roman landscapes it presents, to the water fountains that have been stages of various events and the hotel's swimming pools. On August 5, 1966, the hotel was inaugurated.

While there have not been any wide spread stories about hauntings at Caesar’s there have been a few that are normally told among the staff. It seems that if you go down to the bathrooms in the Forum Casino, the sensor controlled water faucets will turn off and on of their own volition. These are not malfunctions; rather it seems to be intelligently controlled.

Circus Circus

Circus Circus was opened on October 18, 1968 by Jay Sarno, becoming the flagship casino for Circus Circus Enterprises.

Figure 26: Circus Circus Hotel and Casino

At its opening, the $15 million facility only included a casino. Architects Rissman and Rissman Associates designed a giant circus tent shaped main structure, which was built by R.C. Johnson Construction of Las Vegas.

In 1974 ownership changed with the sale of the casino to William Bennett. The facility was expanded with hotel tower additions in 1972, 1980, 1985 and 1986 and 1996 with additional tower renovations following. The hotel's West Tower rooms were renovated to look similar to Excalibur's Widescreen Rooms.

There is a dark side to this gigantic amusement facility. Hotel guests have reported hearing terrifying screams for help coming from the bathrooms in their hotel rooms, which certainly ruins their sleep for the rest of that night. There have also been many cries for help heard coming from the poker room, but no source for these screams can ever be found.

There is another story that years ago three people were murdered in one of the hotel kitchens and their ghosts still roam the hotel/casino looking for their killers. Another sad story comes from room 123 where a young mother, in a fit of depression, killed her young child and then turned the gun on herself. Now the two spirits are seen roaming the hotel looking for the child's father. Sometimes when the woman realizes that someone can see her, she will ask them for help, but she will fade away before anyone can do anything.

Circus Circus is the only hotel on the strip to have an attached Camp Ground of America (KOA) where many RVers park their vehicles while they spend tie in the casino. Many of these guests report that when they have returned to their vehicles to rest that they hear strange sounds coming from outside their vehicles and something will then shake the RV with enough force to rock the occupants. No one has ever seen what might be wandering the campground.

The Excalibur Hotel & Casino

The Excalibur opened on June 19, 1990, originally built by the Circus Circus Company. It featured a prominent, large swimming pool. When it opened it was the largest hotel in the world.

On March 21, 2003, the largest Megabucks Jackpot, as of that time, was hit at the Excalibur. The jackpot was for $39,713,982.25.

On April 26, 2005, the Excalibur, along with the other hotels of the Mandalay Resort Group, was purchased by rival MGM Resorts International.

Figure 27: The Excalibur

Since 2007, most of the medieval themed statues and scenery have been removed. A "garage sale" and auction were held to sell the statues. To this day, few of the wall murals and statues still remain.

While there are no definitive ghosts that have been seen haunting the hallways of the Excalibur, there have been a number of stories told by visitors and guests about hearing whispers in their ears, voices so low that they can't understand the words, but they know something is being said to them. Many others report feeling that there is someone following them, but when they turn, no one is there.

Flamingo Hotel and Casino

Back in the heyday of the mafia, famous gangsters literally flocked to Las Vegas. Benjamin "Bugsy" Siegel, in particular, saw the potential of this gambling mecca, and persuaded his mafia bosses to invest in the most luxurious hotel and casino the area had ever seen. The cost to build The Flamingo ended up being more than three times the original estimate, and despite a glamorous grand opening, the casino was a flop.

Figure 28: Monument to Benjamin Siegel at the

The Flamingo started to turn a nice profit just a few months later, but the Crime Syndicate never forgave Bugsy for embezzling its money to build it. While relaxing in his Beverly Hills home on the evening of June 20, 1947, Bugsy was shot once in the head and four times in the body.

Though much of the original Flamingo he helped to build is no longer in existence, Bugsy's ghost is said to remain, haunting the Presidential Suite, where he resided while in the city. Sightings have also been reported by the pool, in the wedding chapel, and around the Bugsy Monument in The Flamingo's rose garden. A youthful dead Elvis is said to haunt the Flamingo Hilton. Also, any Mafia enthusiast can tell you who Bugsy Siegal was. The man who took a dusty little isolated town named Las Vegas, Nevada and turned it into a gambling metropolis, was snuffed out in his girlfriend's Beverly Hills home in 1947. Bugsy's hotel, The Flamingo, is a throwback to the infancy of sin city. Opened in 1946, the hotel hemorrhaged money its first year, thus bringing about Bugsy's untimely demise. Sprinkled with Bugsy Siegel memorial plaques and artwork, the casino is still a place where Bugsy is said to visit on occasion.

Las Vegas Hilton

Both the land as well as the building at the Las Vegas Hilton have a most interesting history. The land that the hotel sits upon was occupied in the 1950s by the Las Vegas Park Speedway, a failed horse and automobile racing facility. The venture had great potential, but there were a number of factors that worked against success.

On September 4, 1953 the track was opened under the name of the Las Vegas Jockey Club. Ticket booths and tote boards did not work properly and only one entrance discouraged customers. Customers had to wait one hour in

Figure 29: The Las Vegas Hilton

traffic to park and some went home without attending. 8200 customers attended in the first day and the board of directors closed the track for two weeks after the third day to replace the ticket booths. The track was rapidly losing money, so the board closed after operating 13 days. It opened back up in 1954 to host quarter horse racing but closed after seven weeks.

The hotel, designed by architect Martin Stern, Jr., was built in 1969 by Kirk Kerkorian and opened as the International Hotel. When it opened, the International was the largest hotel in the world. Barbra Streisand was the opening-night performer, along with Peggy Lee performing afterwards in the hotel's lounge.

In 1969, right after Streisand's engagement, Elvis Presley performed for 58 consecutive sold out shows, breaking all Vegas attendance records, (130,157 paying, and ostensibly gambling customers in the period of one month), with stellar reviews coming from both critics and the public. He broke his own attendance record in February 1970, and again in August 1970, and August 1972. When playing Las Vegas, he lived in the penthouse suite (room 3000), located on the 30th floor, until his last performance there in December 1976. Elvis was due to perform there again in 1978, to celebrate the opening of the North tower, but the singer died in August 1977. His manager, Colonel Tom Parker, lived in the hotel on the 4th floor from the 1970s to mid-1980s. As we shall see later, Elvis did not leave the building.

Liberace headlined in the showroom during the 1970s drawing sold-out crowds twice per night. When he signed his contract at the Hilton in 1972 he earned $300,000 per week, a record amount for individual entertainers in Las Vegas. He is also said to roam the corridors of this historic old hotel.

The Las Vegas Hilton was the site in 1978 where Leon Spinks defeated Muhammad Ali for the World Heavyweight Championship. It was also the site in which Mike Tyson defeated Tony Tucker to unify and become the Undisputed Heavyweight Champion in 1986. Also, Donald Curry defeated Milton McCrory at the Las Vegas Hilton to unify and become the Undisputed Welterweight Champion in December of 1985.

The International Hotel was sold to Hilton Hotels Corporation in 1970 and renamed the Las Vegas Hilton in 1971. In 1998, Hilton Hotels Corporation split their properties and stock into two different companies (Hilton gaming, and Hilton Hotels). Shortly after the split, Hilton Gaming Company merged with Bally Entertainment

Corporation (owners of Bally's Hotel). The company was re-named Park Place Entertainment. In 2000, Park Place Entertainment purchased Caesars World (All Caesars Casinos). In 2003 Park Place Entertainment changed their name to Caesars Entertainment. In 2004, Caesars Entertainment sold the Las Vegas Hilton to Colony Capital LLC for $280 million. Colony Capital transferred the property to Resorts International Holdings, a Colony Capital company also known as Resorts International. The Las Vegas Hilton is now Resorts International anchor property, with their corporate office located on the second floor of the east tower.

The east tower was added in 1975 and the north tower was added in 1978. Formerly The International Hotel (not to be confused with the Flamingo Hilton) the Las Vegas Hilton boasts the 30th floor "Elvis Presley Suite", which is, of course, haunted by a dead Elvis - this one sporting one of his signature leather studded jumpsuits. He has been seen backstage in the theatre where she performed for so many years and on the freight elevator which he normally took to reach his rooms.

Luxor Hotel and Casino

The Luxor is located on the southern end of the Las Vegas Strip, opposite the McCarran International Airport. The resort is flanked by the Mandalay Bay to the south and by the Excalibur to the north; all three are connected by free express and local trams. All three properties were

Figure 30: The Luxor

built by Circus Circus Enterprises, which later became Mandalay Resort Group.

When it opened on October 15, 1993, the pyramid was the tallest building on the strip and took 2 years to build and a total of 968 workers; it cost $375 million to build. A theater and two additional hotel towers totaling 2,000 rooms were added in 1998 for $675 million. In June 2004, the Mandalay Resort Group was purchased by MGM Resorts International, adding this hotel to its vast array of properties on the "Strip".

When the resort opened, it featured a river that encircled the casino with a ferry that would carry guests to different parts of the pyramid. After guests complained that the ferry service took too long, it was turned into the Nile River Tour, a river ride that passed by many pieces of ancient artwork. Most of the ancient Egypt theme and the river ride were taken away as part of a campaign to tailor the property towards more upscale tastes in 1995.

The resort has been home to some popular entertainment attractions in the Las Vegas area. The main level featured the nightclub, RA, which closed indefinitely on July 22, 2006. From 2000 to 2005, the Luxor Theatre was the home of the enormously popular performance-art show Blue Man Group, which has since moved to The Venetian. On February 15, 2006, the main theater became the home of the musical Hairspray which ran until 2006.

In 2006, MGM-Mirage began completely remodeling Luxor. Rooms in the East and West Towers have been refurnished. Two upscale restaurants, Isis and Sacred Sea Room, closed. This space became CatHouse. The RA nightclub was shuttered. Replacing it is the Las Vegas branch of LAX, a Los Angeles nightclub, which opened on August 31, 2007, in an event hosted by Britney Spears. The Luxor Steakhouse was renovated and reopened as Tender Steak & Seafood. The IMAX Theater is now used to host a human body's exhibition and an exhibition on the RMS Titanic.

There have been a number of stories told about strange happenings inside this unique hotel. Too many people talk about strange and unusual happenings for there not to be something unusual at work.

On May 7, 2007, a vehicle exploded in a Luxor Hotel parking garage, killing an employee. Local authorities believe the victim was the intended target. The hotel was not evacuated, and the parking structure was undamaged. Ongoing investigations show that the explosion was probably caused by a homemade bomb. While the case has not been solved, the spirit of the victim has been seen to return to the parking garage, continually making his rounds.

The next story deals with one of the first mega attractions on the strip, the "Nile River Tour".

The Mirage

The Mirage was built by developer Steve Wynn and designed by Joel Bergman. It opened in November 1989 and was the first resort that was built with the money of Wall Street through the use of junk bonds. It was built on the site, formerly occupied by the Castaways and previous to that, the Red Rooster Nite Club.

The Mirage was the most expensive hotel-casino in history, with a construction cost of US$630 million. The hotel's distinctive gold windows get their color from actual gold dust used in the tinting process. It was reported that the resort would have to bring in a million dollars a day to pay off a 7-year construction loan. But in fact The Mirage

Figure 31: The Mirage Hotel and Casino

did so well, the loan was paid off in just 18 months.

Its construction is also considered very noteworthy in that Wynn had set a new standard for Vegas resorts, and is widely considered to be the father of today's Las Vegas. Prior to The Mirage's opening, the city was experiencing a decline in tourism that began in the 70s, especially around the time that the state of New Jersey legalized gambling and tourists (in particular those on the East Coast) began to frequent the casinos of Atlantic City. Also, this was a time when Las Vegas was no longer considered a fashionable destination, so a new, high-profile, project was necessary to jump-start the ailing industry. When it opened, The Mirage was the first casino to use security cameras full time on all table games.

The site of the Mirage was the original site of the Castaways Hotel & Casino and before the Castaways the

Figure 32: The Mirage Sign

Red Rooster Nite Club sat on the property. The Red Rooster burned in 1931 but it was rebuilt and the San Souci Auto Court was built next door. In 1957 a hotel was added to the property. In 1967 the property became the Castaways which was bought by Howard Hughes in 1970.

From 1990 through 2003, The Mirage was the venue for the Siegfried & Roy show. The two headliners combined magic and the use of wild animals. The closing of the popular attraction in 2003, after Roy Horn was injured by one of the white tigers used in the show, affected The Mirage for a while.

The Mirage's front attraction, the Volcano, erupts regularly at night. In 1993, The Mirage hosted an extended run of the Cirque du Soleil show Nouvelle Expérience in a tent in The Mirage parking lot. It was during this time that Steve Wynn decided to invite Cirque to create Mystère for the soon-to-be-built Treasure Island resort next door. Finally returning to where they began in Las Vegas, Cirque du Soleil has a permanent production at The Mirage, Love.

In 2004, Danny Gans took over the main marquee becoming the resort's main entertainment attraction. In December 2006, the Beatles-themed REVOLUTION ultra-lounge opened. It was the first time Cirque du Soleil was involved in the development of a nightlife venue, operated by Light Group Las Vegas. Gans left The Mirage in 2009 to star in a show at the Encore Las Vegas. In 2009, ventriloquist and 2007 America's Got Talent winner Terry Fator began a 5-year run at the hotel.

Also in 2009, The Mirage was featured on The Amazing Race 15, where one team member had to bungee the other into the air to grab a bouquet of flowers presented in the Love Theater.

But behind the glitz and the glamour there are spirits moving about even in this extremely expensive hotel & Casino. Surprisingly, the stories seem to revolve around the bathroom of what was the Danny Gans Theatre. The automatic sensors on the faucets will turn on and off by themselves at almost any time. The activity is so well known that one cleaning lady refuses to enter the restroom area to clean it and whenever she has cause to get near the restroom she holds her rosary beads in her hand as a shield.

Sahara Hotel & Casino

Figure 33: Sahara Hotel and Casino

The hotel was opened in 1952 by Milton Prell just outside of the City of Las Vegas, and was the sixth resort to open on the Strip. In late 1954, the hotel hired jazz musician Louis Prima to be their late night lounge act, one of the earliest ones on the Las Vegas Strip. Along with his then wife Keely Smith and sax player Sam Butera, they created one of the hottest late night attractions on the Strip. In 1956 Abbott and Costello appeared together for the last time on the Sahara stage before their permanent breakup.

In 1961, the hotel was purchased by Del Webb. In 1962, a Don the Beachcomber restaurant opened in the hotel, becoming a top attraction to not only hotel guests but a variety of celebrities as well. A 24-story tower was added in 1963.

The resort was the site of the annual Jerry Lewis Labor Day Telethon for many years, mostly in the 1970s, and for a brief time in the 1990s.

Performers at the resort over the years have included Frank Sinatra, Dean Martin, Sammy Davis Jr., Judy Garland, Marlene Dietrich, Paul Anka, Liza Minnelli, Violetta Villas, Shirley Bassey, Imogene Coca, Connie Francis, Bill Cosby, Jeanette MacDonald, Ann-Margret, Joey Bishop, Don Rickles, Bobby Darin, and many others.

Del Webb ran into financial problems in the late 1970s and early 1980s, sold the Sahara to Paul Lowden (Archon Corporation) for $50 million in 1982.

Ownership changed in 1995 when Archon Corporation sold the property to Bill Bennett. Bill Bennett owned the hotel until his death on December 22, 2002. The property has since been owned by the Bill Bennett Family Trust.

The 27-story tower addition was added in 1987 and a new porte-cochere was added by the relocated pool in 1997.

In 1999 further renovations added a roller coaster and the NASCAR restaurant. The roller coaster, called Speed-The Ride, shoots riders from the hotel outside along the Las Vegas Strip, where it loops through the grandiose Sahara sign in front of the hotel, goes straight up, stops and then takes a return trip backwards. Bergman Walls Associates were the 1999 architects.

Rumors of the Sahara's closure surfaced in the media in February 2006. In a news article on June 30, 2006, it was reported that the Sahara site, as well as a defunct adjacent Wet 'n Wild property, were for sale.

On March 2, 2007, Sam Nazarian and Stockbridge Real Estate Group signed an agreement to purchase the Sahara from the Bennett family. The transaction is said to be valued between $300 and $400 million for just the hotel/casino and its 17.45-acre (7.06 ha) lot. The deal does not include the 26-acre (11 ha) lot across the Strip from the Sahara and 11-acre (4.5 ha) lot east of the Sahara on Paradise Road. Nazarian's current plans are for Navegante Management Group, current operators of the downtown casinos The Plaza, The Western, The Vegas Club, and The Gold Spike, to run the Sahara's casino while Nazarian's SBE Hotel Group will manage the hotel and Nazarian's SBE Restaurant and Nightlife Group manages its food and beverage operations.

The first ghost took up residence just after the 24 story tower was added to the hotel making it the tallest hotel in the western United States. What was a marvel to many was a way to end it all to others. A man who had gone through a very bad run of bad luck went to the Sahara early one morning and went up to the top floor. Security chased him off three different times, but he was determined and he returned to the top of the tower a fourth time. After sitting and looking at the sunrise for a time, he jumped to his death. Now many visitors and guests report feeling someone come up to them and whisper in their ear. They can't understand what he is saying, but this feeling will continue for several minutes. Maybe he is asking for someone to talk him out of ending it all.

Sun Coast Hotel and Casino

The Suncoast Hotel and Casino is a local's casino

Figure 34: Suncoast Hotel and Casino

and hotel in Las Vegas, Nevada, owned by Boyd Gaming Corporation. The hotel, located on a 50 acres (20 ha) site, contains 432 rooms and has an 82,000-square-foot (7,600 m2) casino (with over 2000 slot machines) as well as a Century group movie theatre, bowling alley, and conference room/meeting space.

The Suncoast is sometimes listed as being in Summerlin, but it is not a part of Summerlin. It is located next to Summerlin. When it was built, the tower was the tallest structure on the west side of the Las Vegas Valley. The hotel and casino opened on September 12, 2000, with a five-minute, $75,000 fireworks show. It was built by Michael Gaughan's Coast Resorts, hence the Suncoast moniker (Coast was purchased by Boyd Gaming in 2004).

At the time, it was expected that as many as 90 percent of the property's customers would be local Las Vegas residents rather than out of town tourists.

The bowling alley was officially renamed "The Swap" in honor of Skunk Ape's visit on November 10, 2007.

Tropicana Hotel and Casino

The original building, with the Garden room wings, was built in 1957. The Paradise Tower, consisting of 22 floors of guest rooms and suites, was built in 1979 as the Tiffany Tower, adjoining the resort's Tiffany Theatre, until March 28, 2009 home to the Follies Bergère production show. A 21-story Island Tower was constructed in 1986.

Figure 35: Tropicana

In May 2006, Tropicana Entertainment, LLC acquired the Tropicana Resort & Casino Las Vegas from then publicly-traded Aztar Corporation for approximately $2.1 billion in cash. The acquisition was approved by the Nevada Gaming Commission on November 17, 2006 and was completed in December of that year.

On May 15, 2009 it was reported by the Las Vegas Sun and Forbes that Canadian investment firm Onex Corporation will take control of the Tropicana Resort and Casino in Las Vegas from Tropicana Entertainment when it emerges from bankruptcy later this year. Alex Yemenidjian who previously served as CEO of both the MGM Mirage Resort Company and Metro-Goldwyn-Mayer movie studio under Kirk Kerkorian's ownership has been tapped by Onex to be the Las Vegas Strip resort's new CEO and oversee the casino's day to day operations.

Tropicana Las Vegas Hotel and Resort Inc. is the company formed by Onex in which it has the controlling interest but it has several equity partners. Tropicana Las Vegas Inc. owns the property.

Union Plaza Hotel and Casino -

The Union Plaza Hotel, now called the Plaza Hotel and Casino, was built at the site of the former downtown train station. Some say the showroom of the hotel is haunted by the ghost of a stagehand who committed suicide years ago. Perhaps regretting his final decision once the deed was done, this ghost is said to hang around, playing pranks on those who remain in his former environment. His hallmark, besides the occasional cold spot, is misplacing people's belongings.

A few of those who work the showroom insist the restless soul is the spirit of the great Houdini himself. And since the magic show held here is a tribute to Houdini's talents as an escape artist and magician, maybe they're right. He could be sticking around to make sure everything is done just right. The showgirls at this Fremont Street casino are haunted by the ghost of a lighting man who killed himself years ago. They say he lurks in the corners of their dressing rooms "a cloud like figure", and tampers with the shows. Lights will blink, staff states, during performances. One staff said she saw someone in the lighting booth when she returned to the stage to pick something up very late at night. Upon investigating, the booth was empty, even though someone would've had to pass by her to leave the area.

Figure 36: Plaza Hotel & Casino

Harry Houdini is said to mess with stage hands during Houdini enthusiast Dixie Dooley's recreations of Houdini's tricks at the casino. They have reported people shoving them through the curtains, only to find no one there.

Whiskey Pete's Casino

The area now known as Whiskey Pete's was originally owned by an old, cranky gas station owner named Pete MacIntyre. Pete was a small scale jack of all trades who was into a number of activities. According to local rumor, Pete apparently had a difficult time making ends meet selling gas so he resorted to a little bootlegging. From this off the books business, he gained the nickname of "Whiskey Pete".

Figure 37: Whiskey Pete's Casino

When Whiskey Pete died of miners' lung in 1933, legend has it that he wanted to be buried standing up with a bottle of bootleg in his hands so he could continue to watch over the area that had been his property.

According to legend, his friend set out to dig a hole to hold an upright coffin but gave up before they finished. So he was buried sort of sideways.

Whiskey Pete's unmarked grave was accidentally exhumed while workers were building a connecting bridge from Whiskey Pete's to Buffalo Bill's (on the other side of I-15). The body was moved and is now said to be buried in one of the caves where Pete cooked up his moonshine.

Pete's ghost has been spotted wandering around the casino that bears his name. He plays with the light switches, knocks over glasses in the kitchen, and pulls off bed covers. There have also been stories of visitors arriving at the hotel with their gas tanks on empty only to find their fuel gauges showing the tank is full when they get in their cars the next morning, courtesy of Pete.

Whiskey Pete's was opened in 1977 by Ernest Jay Primm as the first of the casinos to be located at what was then called Stateline.

In 1983, a new hotel tower was constructed as part of an expansion of the property.

Whiskey Pete's used to have a display of the Bonnie and Clyde car, but it has since been moved across the I-15 freeway to the newly redesigned Primm Valley Resort.

The Mapes Hotel

The Mapes Hotel and Casino was the first major high-rise hotel built in this country after World War II. When the twelve-story Mapes Hotel opened in the heart of Reno in December 1947, it was the tallest building in Nevada. The hotel was significant in the development of the tourism industry and was the forerunner of the Nevada casino-hotels built specifically to offer gaming, guest accommodations, restaurants, bars, and big name entertainment.

Figure 38: Mapes Hotel from a postcard found in Reno

The property was named after a prominent Reno family. The Mapes Hotel and Casino was the first major high-rise hotel built in this country after World War II. When the twelve-story Mapes Hotel opened in the heart of Reno in December 1947, it was the tallest building in Nevada. The hotel was significant in the development of the tourism industry and was the forerunner of the Nevada casino-hotels built specifically to offer gaming, guest accommodations, restaurants, bars, and big name entertainment.

The property was named after a prominent Reno family. Early settlers George W. Mapes and his brother, Ira, ran cattle through the Truckee Meadows in the 1860s. After George died, his son, Charles Mapes, Sr., planned to build an elegant hotel as a monument to his late father.

Charles, Sr. and his wife, Gladys, purchased the "old" federal office building and post office property on the

southeast

Figure 39: The Mapes Hotel

corner of North Virginia and First Streets on the north bank of the Truckee River in 1937. When World War II ended, Charles Mapes, Jr. and his family decided to build their dream hotel using the blueprints chosen by Charles, Sr. and Gladys. Architect F. H. Slocombe from Oakland, California, designed the hotel, while Theodore P. Moorehead, civil engineer, managed its construction.

Construction began in January 1946, but the shortage of materials after the war delayed the process. The Mapes officially opened on December 17, 1947. The estimated costs to complete the deluxe hotel ranged from $2,500,000 to $3,000,000.

The building was erected using reinforced concrete in a curtain column and plate floor style of construction. None of the exterior walls was weight-bearing. With fire safety in mind, the rooms were built without transoms, and all moldings, window sashes, and baseboards were made of aluminum. The grained, hollow, metal doors and the plaster-covered terra cotta column walls were intended to contain any fire to a single living unit with a four-hour fire resistance rating.

The hotel-casino building contained about 147,500 square feet with the basement and first two stories being larger than the upper floors. The first two floors of the exterior of the hotel were covered with four-by-four, cream-colored, tiles that resembled terra cotta. Roughly textured red brick columns rose between the windows of the upper stories. The lobby featured the hotel registration desk and the three elevators with operators. No other structure in Nevada had as many elevators as the Mapes.

The eight residential floors were advertised to contain 300 rooms as well as forty suites—each with a living room, dining room, kitchen, bedroom, and tiled bathroom. Three corner suites were unique because the corridor could be closed off and up to five additional bedrooms added to those suites. (Marilyn Monroe stayed in a corner suite during most of the filming of the Misfits.) The standard guest room had a window and was only about the size of a single-car garage. The rooms were each designed to accommodate a single twin bed, which served as a sofa during the day.

The Sky Room, a cosmopolitan nightclub, was located on the top floor. At the time, only a few hotels in the country offered dining, dancing, and floor shows on their top floors. The Sky Room kitchen was capable of serving as many as 400 people at one meal; lunch and dinner were served daily. Sky Room patrons had unobstructed views of the southwest sections of Reno, the rippling blue river, the foothills, and the Sierra Nevada.

Gaming was offered either on the main floor or on the top floor outside the Sky Room. The guests also had a choice of two bars for liquid refreshments, either in the cocktail lounge on the main floor or in the Sky Room bar.

Provocative entertainment and famous show business personalities drew guests to the hotel. A few of the better-known entertainers included the comedic team of the Marx Brothers; singers Vic Damone, Judy Garland and Tony Bennett; pianist Liberace; and burlesque dancer Gypsy Rose Lee. During the Squaw Valley Winter

Olympics in 1960, Sammy Davis, Jr. debuted as the lead singer, with his father and uncle, in the Will Mastin Trio. In addition, Charles Mapes sponsored sporting events to promote the hotel, such as the Reno Rodeo, golf tournaments, and hydroplane races.

In the summer of 1978, Mapes borrowed heavily for an expansion of his Money Tree Casino on North Virginia and Sierra Streets. He could not compete with the new major hotel-casinos that had opened that summer, such as the Sahara Reno, Circus Circus, and MGM Grand Hotel-Casino. In December 1982, when Mapes was unable to repay the $15 million he had borrowed, the bank foreclosed—not only on the Money Tree, but also on the Mapes Hotel. In June 1988, George Karadanis and Robert Maloff, partners in the Sundowner Hotel, bought the Mapes. Without having opened or improved the building, the new owners sold the hotel to the Reno Redevelopment Agency in 1996.

In September 1999, the Reno City Council voted to demolish the hotel, in spite of the objections of area preservationists and historians. Clauss Construction imploded the hotel on a wintry Super Bowl Sunday morning, January 30, 2000. It was the first building on the

National Register of Historic Places to be demolished since 1949.

The Mapes was a demure counter to the gaudy casinos down the street. Instead of beads of blinking lights running up and down its facade, it has concrete panels in bas relief. Instead of a riot of neon on the roof, it has an Art Deco zigzag cornice.

The Mapes Hotel was a grand beauty of a building prominently located near the Truckee River. In addition to its numerous other attractions, it was long reported to be haunted for decades by an unknown spirit. After the hotel was torn down, the same presence has been reported lingering near the ice rink on the spot of the old hotel that is set up in the winter months.

INDEX

2

3

4

A

B

C

D

E

F

G

H

S

T

U

V

W

CPSIA information can be obtained at www.ICGtesting.com
Printed in the USA
LVOW07s2230200616

493349LV00020B/933/P